PRAISE FO

"*The Burn Zone* is a remarkable read that is sure to pull at your heartstrings. A story that will stay with you long after reading."

—Lovely Loveday book reviewer

"Easily the best memoir I've ever read."

—*Book Recon*

"My main takeaway from this book and Linnell as a writer is how incredibly strong and brilliant she is."

—*The Plucky Reader*

"Renee did such an amazing job with this book. If there is one memoir I think you need to read right away—this is the one!! Not only is her story just amazing, but her writing of her story is beyond excellent."

—*Writing Fun*'s Michelle Dunton

"This page-turner of a memoir is part cautionary tale, part inspirational story that speaks volumes about what makes people human and their longing to belong. The language is down to earth and easy to understand without any complicated meditation terms to learn. She simply tells her story in the hopes of inspiring others to live their true self. *The Burn Zone* is recommended for readers who appreciate memoirs with spiritual and meditation themes."

—*SA Examiner*

"Linnell describing her depression felt like I was reading parts of my own life in the last few years. If you've ever wanted to know what is going on with a loved one while they suffer from depression, I can't recommend this book enough. It's raw and powerful and it's true. And the way out of depression is also true. It's not a quick process and if you want to know more, definitely read this book."

—*Tea, Chocolate, and Books*

"As she winds her way out of the insanity of two people who have kept her in thrall, Renee discovers she is stronger than she thinks. Beautifully done."

—*Mrs. Mommy Booknerd*

"Renee's comeback, reclamation and finally accepting herself for what she is provides for quite an engaging read. She has an easy, believable writing style that makes you think she is talking directly to you in a private conversation. *The Burn Zone* definitely spoke to me, and the self-help benefits should do wonders for anyone else who gives this book a try."

—*Bookreporter*

"Renee's transparency is what made this memoir real. There was no sugarcoating. She told it like it was."

—*This Mom's Delight*

"This book truly was something else. Reading about Renee's journey was heartbreaking, addicting, inspiring, and so much more. I enjoyed this memoir and recommend it to those who seek spiritual Enlightenment."

—*Lauren's Bookshelf*

"Heartbreaking as it is, this is a most important book."

—*Phil Jason Reviews*

"Memoir offers lost souls a viable path to self-respect and renewal."

—*The Florida Weekly*

"I cheered Renee on from the start. She finds purpose in her life right before the reader's eyes, and what's more relatable than that? I was captivated by the story and emotional at different points due to the author's brutal honesty and vulnerability. Overall, I found *The Burn Zone* an impressive and memorable memoir, one that will stick with me."

—*The Tar Heel Reader*

STILL ON FIRE

RENEE LINNELL

STILL ON FIRE

a memoir

Pink Skeleton
— PUBLISHING —

Pink Skeleton Publishing, Inc.
625 E Main Street, STE 104
Aspen, CO 81611

ORDERING INFORMATION
Quantity sales. Special discounts are available on quantity purchases by corporations, associations, and others. For details, contact the «Special Sales Department» at the address above.
Orders by US trade bookstores and wholesalers. Please contact BCH (800) 431-1579 or visit http://www.bookch.com for details.

Printed in the United States of America

Cataloging-in-Publication Data

Names: Linnell, Renee, author.
Title: Still on fire : a memoir / Renee Linnell.
Description: Aspen, CO: Pink Skeleton Publishing, 2022.
Identifiers: LCCN: 2022909398 | ISBN: 979-8-9861647-3-1
Subjects: LCSH Linnell, Renee. | Self-actualization (Psychology) | Self-realization. | Women--Biography. | Self-help. | BISAC BIOGRAPHY & AUTOBIOGRAPHY / Personal Memoirs | SELF-HELP / Personal Growth / Self-Esteem
Classification: LCC HQ1206 .L56 2022 | DDC 155.633092--dc23

Interior design by Mimi Bark
Names and identifying characteristics have been changed to protect the privacy of certain individuals.

When you walk to the edge of all the light you have and take
that first step into the darkness of the unknown, you must believe
one of two things will happen: there will be something solid for
you to stand upon or you will be taught how to fly.

—PATRICK OVERTON

To everyone who is tired—
tired of fitting in, tired of playing small,
tired of being afraid, overworked, overstressed . . .
and tired of living a life without true joy.
May you stop making excuses for why mediocrity
is okay for you and take the leap into a life that you love.

Contents

Part 1: Decisions

Part 2: Wild Ride

Part 3: Spirit

Part 4: Love

Part 5: Whole

Don't ask what the world needs. Ask what makes you come alive, and go do it. Because what the world needs is people who have come alive.

—HOWARD THURMAN

PReFace

We think we want to see the entire future. We think we want to know all the steps and turns in the path ahead. But the truth is that would bore us and make life not worth living.

It really is so much more fun to follow our desires, listen to our Inner Guidance, and take the next right step, then the next right step, and then the next right step, not knowing where each step will lead but trusting that it is going to lead to someplace amazing, where we can learn and grow from all our "mistakes" and enjoy all the beautiful gifts offered along the way. Trusting that if we cannot see the next right step, we are not yet meant to, and until the step becomes clear, our job is to find a way to enjoy the present. When we find gratitude and joy in the present, we lift our vibration to one of Light, and with that Light the next step always becomes clear.

This is true happiness. This is living happily ever after. It's being present in and appreciating all the tiny moments that we miss *right now* when we're continuously looking forward to living a happy life.

By the time I was twenty-seven, I had been to twenty-seven countries and slept with twenty-seven men. I stopped counting both countries and men when I hit fifty of each. When I was thirty-three I joined a Buddhist cult, where I was severely brainwashed; I burned almost everything I owned and lost my friends, my sanity, and almost my life. When I was thirty-nine I went into business with a guy I met in a karate dojo in New York. I knew him for only six months. I had no operating agreement. And I ended up embroiled in a huge lawsuit, losing hundreds of thousands of dollars, and smeared all over the New York tabloids. My mother drowned in a bathtub when I was twenty-nine. My father died on Thanksgiving Day when I was fifteen. Most of the rest of my family died before that. I endured my share of trauma; I stuffed down my share of shame.

We shouldn't be afraid of our stories. We shouldn't be afraid of our voice. And we shouldn't see anything that happened to us as "wrong." We are in these human bodies for such a brief period of time. When we incarnated, we signed up for a wild ride. Why spend any moment of it afraid? Why hide who we are? Why limit ourselves? Why numb our emotions with addiction? Each one of us is God/Goddess expressing uniquely through *our own* unique form. We are the *only* expression of us there is. Once we are gone, this unique expression is lost. What are we waiting for?

The time to live is *now*. Our life is *now*. It is all the tiny moments we are *missing* as we keep waiting for life to start. It is all the opportunities to love that we miss because we shut our hearts down in fear. It is all the opportunities to *live* that we miss because crusty old belief systems tell us "we can't." Life only feels "over in a flash" if we keep postponing joy and love for a later date, living the same day repeatedly, sacrificing what could be fresh and miraculous and alive and new for the "safe" and "predictable" and mundane.

Imagine a world where we are courageous enough to be ourselves, to speak our truth, knowing we have a unique and important perspective to add. Where we are bold enough to go after the deepest desires of our heart, knowing our desires are unique to us and planted in our heart by the Hand of the Divine. Where we understand we add our Light to the sum of Light when we stand tall in who we are. Unafraid. Unashamed.

We are guided more than we know. Protected so much more than we could ever realize. We spend so much of our lives worried about what other people think of us, worried about being hurt, worried about dying. Death doesn't just come for us randomly. We don't just die for no reason. We die when we have either fulfilled our purpose here on Earth and are ready to move on or when we have decided we no longer wish to be here and we want to return Home. Either way, death is not something to fear. It is a transition back to the pure Light from whence we came. It is a supreme graduation to the next level.

These moments spent worrying are precious moments we can never get back; they are precious life force energy wasted. Worry is using our mind energy to create a future we dread. Why are we not taught this as children? Why are we not taught how destructive this is? We are taught to feel shame regarding the most magical parts of our human body. We are taught we cannot make money doing what we love. We are taught that we are not okay as we are and have to change to please the adults around us. We are taught so much lack-consciousness and so much restriction. Rarely are we taught to truly be ourselves and follow our dreams.

I heard once that when trying to decide between two options, always pick the one that will leave the better story. I have tried to do that my entire life.

Mary Oliver, in her magnificent poem "West Wind #2," tells us to put down our oars and trust the stream of life to carry us. She says only when we hear the water slamming against the jagged rocks, when we "feel the mist on [our] mouth and sense ahead the embattlement, the long falls plunging and steaming" should we then pick up our oars and "row, row for [our] life toward it."

Row for our life *toward* it. Toward what gets our heart racing. Toward what makes us nervous. Toward what gets the lifeblood pumping.

We are blessed, magical beings. We came here specifically to experience life on Earth in human bodies. We are not meant to be so afraid. All the mystics, saints, and shamans say we are Source Energy, expressing uniquely as each one of us. We spend so much of our childhood trying to fit in, trying to please the adults around us, trying to blend in with the other kids and be popular. We forget who we are. It is time to remember.

This is the only way life on Earth gets better, for all of us. Haven't you noticed we are drawn to people who are authentic? Think of those people who dance horribly and with total abandon at weddings. We all *love* them! They give us permission to get up and dance horribly ourselves. Think of the super-tan, leather-skinned, wrinkly old man Rollerblading down the sidewalk in a neon Speedo. He makes us smile ear to ear in his eccentricity. We *love* seeing this man as we drive by.

The people we admire the most are those who are completely, unapologetically themselves. The people who have created the most fantastic lives for themselves are people who went against the norm and initially got demonized and ostracized but stayed true to their own understanding of who they were, refusing to compromise. Think of Prince in his high heels and his tiny underpants, prancing around, singing about purple rain. He tried to start his career as an opening band but got booed off the stage. Instead of hanging his head in shame and quitting, he knew immediately he was not meant to be an opening act. He knew in his heart he was a headliner. And he refused to open for anyone else ever again. He was the main event.

Authenticity is magnetic. Authenticity is the true essence of Source animating the expression of each one of us, unimpeded by self-doubt, confusion, or shame. We resist being around people who pull on our energy for attention, love, and validation. And we are in awe of those who stand strongly on their own two feet, believing in themselves, not needing us for validation.

So many people are trying to save the world, change the world. But that has to start with saving ourselves. And we do this by getting to know our self, our *authentic* self. Not what the media tells us we are supposed to be. Not what our parents and teachers and religious leaders tell us we are supposed to be. What the tiny, quiet voice inside tells us. The child inside us. The one who knows what we love, in which endeavors we excel, what we were born to do. Each one of us is born with unique gifts, the parts of ourselves we tried to hide as children because they made us different—these are the keys to unlocking our destiny. We must uncover them. Dust them off. Give them love. Nurture them. Develop them. And wear them with pride.

Our skin color is not wrong. Our body size and shape are not wrong. Our ethnicity is not a mistake. Our sexual preference is not a mistake. Our accent, our wounds, our traumas, our "deformities," none of these are mistakes. We *chose*—our soul *chose*—every single experience, every single part of our physical form, in order for us to learn what we came here to learn and teach what we came here to teach. It *chose* the just-right upbringing and the just-right experiences and the just-right physical form to fulfill our destiny here on Earth. Isn't that something to get excited about?

We need you, *as you*, here, now, expressing yourself fully. Trusting yourself. Trusting the ways you are different. Do not be afraid. Do not be ashamed. We need the lessons you have learned from the "mistakes" you have made or the traumas you have endured.

I spent most of my life feeling like an alien here on Earth. Feeling *so incredibly different.* I could blend in, but I never truly fit. And then one day I realized I felt like a caged dragon. I felt like an intense, winged, fire-breathing being stuck in a container that made me hide my wings and my ability to breathe fire, because my size and my wings and my intensity scared people. It was only when *The Burn Zone* was published and my story was in black-and-white for the whole world to read that I realized I was done hiding, that hiding was killing me. I decided to spread my wings, to shatter my cage, and to *roar* with fire . . . I decided to estrange everyone who liked me small. It was terrifying. And it left me almost alone for a stretch. But the more I stayed true to myself, the more those who didn't love the true me left and the more space I created around myself for those who loved me *as me* to enter.

It's hard to go against the norm. We risk being ostracized and demonized. We risk being misunderstood. But spending our lives locked in a cage is worse.

I implore you: Begin unfolding those wings. Begin playing with your own fire. Begin testing how high and how far you can soar. Because only when we are willing to expand and roar can other similar beings find us. Only in our authenticity can we finally feel not-all-alone. Only as our *true self* will we ever see where and how we fit into the divine tapestry called life. Let's not wait one moment more.

INtRODUCtiON

We're standing outside a hotel in Florida. It's close to 2:00 a.m., and the air is hot and thick and humid, smelling like wet earth, grass, and trees from the recent downpour of rain. We can hear music and laughter from the bars nearby. I'm wearing light-blue skinny jeans and a flowery pale-yellow off-the-shoulder top, blousy in the sleeves and tight around my torso. My camel-colored wedge heels are dangling from my right hand; I had removed them to walk from the bar to the hotel.

My left hand is interlocked with his, our fingers intertwined; the side of my face is level with his shoulder. We're both sweaty from dancing, and I'm drunk. All the tequila is just now starting to hit me, and as we walk, I begin to swerve and my world starts to spin. He notices and stops walking. He turns to face me. And then he leans down to kiss me. A beautiful kiss. Slow and soft, caring and full of passion and presence . . . and love. My knees go weak, and my world spins a little more.

As I lose myself in the kiss and the magic of the moment, I feel fleshy, warm, full lips on the back of my neck. Deliberate kisses working their way from the top of my shoulderless shirt to the base of my skull. Slowly. Sensuously.

7

His friend, who had been walking beside us. His *incredibly* handsome friend. Tan skin, long blond hair, beautiful white smile, super fun on the dance floor, wild and sexy and athletically built. The man who had been lap-dancing me. The man who had been buying me extra shots of expensive tequila. His best friend. Kissing me at the same time from behind. They are both much younger than I am by something close to twenty years. They are both professional tennis players. They are both *incredibly* handsome and healthy and thriving in life. And they both clearly appreciate older women.

Suddenly I understand how far I've come. How much I've grown. How *completely* I have my own back. Because I check in with myself even in my drunken blur.

Do I want this? I ask. *Is this okay?*

As if reading my thoughts, his friend murmurs into my neck, "You are so sexy. Would you like a night of amazing sex?"

I stop kissing the man in front of me. My world is spinning. My book tour ended this morning. Six years of hard work—over. Is this my gift from the Book Tour Gods? Is this how I want to celebrate? I remember the vow I made to my Inner Child, and I ask her if she wants to invite these men inside. As a light mist starts to fall, we all take a step sideways into the shelter of the trees.

PART 1

DECISIONS

The most important decision we will
ever make is whether we believe we live
in a friendly or a hostile universe.

—ALBERT EINSTEIN

CHAPTER 1

SLOW DOWN

I have a confession to make: I'm not very good at being human. I still can't figure it out. For the life of me, I cannot figure out other people, and even after all these years of trying, I can't figure out myself. And maybe that's the whole point. Maybe that's what makes life dynamic and thrilling. I'm not sure. Maybe "I'm not sure" is the answer to all of it.

I have noticed that anytime I think I'm sure, life comes along and proves me wrong. I have noticed that anytime I think I'm sure, I turn into a bit of an asshole. I close my mind to ideas and concepts and people that oppose the way I think I'm sure. And I am really beginning to see how quantum physics is right when it tells us there are billions of simultaneous realities. The Buddha said, "With our thoughts we make the world." Science is finally catching up to what the mystics, saints, and shamans have been saying for thousands of years: our thoughts create our reality. There are billions of us, each with a unique perspective, so there are *billions* of simultaneous realities. No wonder we can't get along.

What if we stopped trying so hard to get others to see from our point of view? What if we finally realized our point of view works for us because it is ours. But everyone else has a point of view that works for each one of them. If it didn't work, they would seek alternative information and change it.

What if life on Earth really is just the ultimate video game? We incarnate in these bodies, and like Dwayne "The Rock" Johnson and the other characters do in the movie *Jumanji*, we have to figure out how our avatars work. We discover our strengths and weaknesses. We learn about our bodies, our flaws, and our unique skill sets. We discover our likes and dislikes. Personal preferences. And we fine-tune as we go.

We get plopped into these bodies and these personalities that are constantly surprising us. And at the same time, we get plopped into a world where every single other human is living in a different reality, looking through a different lens. They are *creating* from a different lens, and with a different skill set, different wants and needs. And then we add that each human is *projecting* that different reality onto everybody else: Thieves think everyone else is stealing from them; lovers think everyone else has good intentions; cheaters think everyone else is cheating; fighters always find people with whom to fight. You get the point.

Combine all that with the fact that when we are young, and often for most of our lives, we bend and mold and shape ourselves into false versions of ourselves to fit in and people-please. And we end up with a shit show. Seriously. It's fascinating.

The only way to unwind the shit show is for each one of us to stop caring so much about what other people think about us, to stop comparing our lives to the lives of others, to start discovering who we truly are, and then to build an authentic life around it. This raises us up, out of the mess, and it washes off the shit so that we *sparkle* with light. If we trust that we are here for a reason, that we are unique for a reason, and that a divine path is already lined up for us, life gets a lot easier. As we admit we do not know, that it is all a mystery, that as soon as we think we have the world or ourselves or anyone else figured out, we get the carpet pulled out from under us—we get our paradigm shattered—life gets a lot more fun. It's like walking up to the River of Life and someone asking, "Where does this river go?" and you answer, "I have no idea, but it sure looks like fun!" and jump in. Arms up in the air. Ready for the ride. *Trusting* that wherever the ride leads is someplace amazing.

This morning I was meditating in my favorite living room chair, and I had a vision of myself in that same chair at about eighty years old. I saw how little and how wrinkled and how wise this version of me was. She was *glowing*. She was so patient, so calm, so *content*. And she offered me advice. She said to me, "Slow down."

Just those two words.

"Slow down."

She sat there in her comfy lounge clothing with her warm cup of coffee, and she was so beautiful in her calm, in her peace, in her wisdom.

"Slow down."

She said, "You will be here in a flash, and you don't want to miss any moment of it." She told me, "It is all coming. All of it. All that you dream about. But it is not your work to do. It is God's work to do through you. If you do not slow down, you cannot be a clear channel. The same way you cannot rush a baby into this world, you cannot rush your accomplishments; they will be born when they are meant to be born, after the proper gestation. Your unique contribution *will* be offered. It must be. But if you rush the process, you end up with a child that does not have fully functioning lungs. So, please, my love, slow down."

CHAPTER 2

DROWNING

I was drowning. I was going to drown. And I was most probably going to be smashed into the lava rocks as it happened. My mind went utterly calm. There was nothing I could do. A lifeguard was going to have to save me, or I was going to die. No real choices on my end. No options left except try to keep air in my lungs a few more seconds at a time.

I was treading water just outside the shore break of Waimea Bay, about fifteen feet from the beach, getting sucked rapidly toward the "Death Zone" (the name the locals endearingly gave the razor-sharp black lava rocks and cliff faces on the west side of the bay). The swell that day was easily twenty feet Hawaiian (close to thirty-five-foot wave faces) with some even bigger sets. The water was a deep turquoise blue, and the swell was rolling in from far across the world, gathering tremendous momentum as it crossed the wide-open expanse. The surf was *huge* and an amazing spectacle to watch. Its power was tangible from up on the road as it thumped and pummeled the shore with a deafening roar, sending massive sprays of salt water high into the air as the waves hit the beach and surrounding cliffs.

I had met Latham, an *incredibly* handsome, well-known Australian big-wave rider the day before, while watching the sunset at Sunset Beach. And in my effort to get to know him better, I had allowed him to talk me into paddling out into the channel with him, on his board, to watch people surf Waimea Bay. I knew better than to do this. I had been raised on a boat by a military father who was captain of a landing craft infantry vessel in five invasions in World War II. He taught me from as early as I could remember to respect the ocean, to understand tides and swells, and to never, *ever* get myself in water I could not handle. But . . . this guy was so *hot*. And he was *such* a good surfer.

And, I reasoned with myself, *he has to know what he's doing; he surfs here all the time*. And did I mention that he was hot? Six feet tall, big blue eyes, golden-brown skin, curly sun-kissed dirty-blond hair, muscles on top of muscles on top of muscles. Built like an Adonis. How could I possibly resist?

So I agreed to go. And I got on the front of his thirteen-foot *rhino chaser* (surfboard for surfing huge waves). And I lay down on my stomach and put my tan, round, bikini-clad bottom in his face, my legs spread slightly so he could lie down behind me, torso between my thighs, chest resting on the curve of my behind. And together we paddled out into the channel, my heart racing the entire time.

A lifeguard on a Jet Ski raced up to us as we were paddling out. "You're not planning to surf, are you?" he asked, concerned.

"No," we responded in unison.

He recognized Latham. "Oh, howzit?" he said, sounding relieved.

"Just going to sit in the channel and watch, mate," Latham said.

"Okay," the lifeguard responded reluctantly, then took off to our left and went out to the lineup as we continued our paddle out.

Latham kept us safely away from where the waves were breaking, and we got to see some *incredible* airdrops by surfers on huge boards—angles and views you simply cannot get from the beach. The energy of the surfers in the lineup was frenzied and passionate. The fear and adrenaline were tangible. The surfers swirled around one another, jockeying for position, those deepest and farthest away from us having priority but also holding the most dangerous positions, with much farther to go to make it to safety once they dropped into a wave and more of a chance that another surfer would drop in on them, blocking their exit into the safety of the shoulder of the wave and the channel beside it. Men were screaming support to one another, hooting and hollering for each surfer that went for it, and yelling in unison when surfers got shot out of the barrels. Lifeguards on Jet Skis were racing from the outside to the inside, constantly scanning for surfers who may need rescue. The buzz of the Jet Skis was barely audible over the roar of the crashing surf. A helicopter was circling above, adding to the noise, photographers hanging out the side doors. I was smack-dab in the middle of one of the best surf spots in the world, surrounded by the best surfers in the world.

But I was afraid. Too afraid to enjoy myself. I knew too much about the ocean. I knew you could never, and *should never*, predict it. You could never, and *should never*, assume in a situation like this that a random rogue sweeper set (bigger set) would not roll through. I didn't care how much he knew about Waimea, about where it would break and where it would not. I was terrified. This was a typical day in the office for Latham; it was toying with death for me. I wanted to go in.

So, after less than ten minutes, I asked to go back to the beach. We turned around and paddled back, my heart thumping in my chest, my body quivering from all the adrenaline, my breath shallow, coming in panicked gasps.

"Okay, now here's the tricky part," Latham said. "I will take us to the beach, and you will have to jump off immediately so the shore-pound doesn't smash us."

"Okay," I responded nervously. And in we went, to the north corner of the bay. Latham had timed it perfectly. I jumped off. I stumbled as a wave hit me from behind. I kept my gaze fixed on the dry sand and heaved my body through the waist-high, churning, foamy, sandy white water. I didn't know what he was doing, and I didn't care. I just wanted to get to the safety of the dry sand. I was trembling, panting, and filled with fear.

My legs did not seem grounded. I could barely gain traction. The swirling water grabbed me by the waist and legs and dragged me backward. I leaned away from it and made it a few steps toward the beach, but then got sucked backward, off the sand, by the water. Sucked off the shore and immediately swept south by the current. Latham was trying to get himself and the thirteen-foot surfboard onto the beach and did not notice. I didn't know what to do. The shore-pound was easily double overhead, smashing with ferocious force onto the sand, and there seemed no pause between waves. I would break into pieces and die if I tried to swim through it to the beach. And yet staying just outside it, I was getting swept toward the lava rocks. *Quickly.*

I made a few attempts to enter the shore-pound and ended up being slammed in circles, airless and choking on water and sand. I gave up. I was going to drown if I kept trying. And my body was quickly tiring from trying to fight the current and from my panicked shallow breathing. I knew I had to relax. I knew people drown because they panic. I knew a relaxed body stays afloat longer. And I prayed a lifeguard would see me. But I was tired. *So* tired. And I estimated I had about four minutes before I got smashed into the rocks.

I had recently been diagnosed with chronic fatigue syndrome. After a six-month around-the-world modeling job, I'd tried to make up for my lost semester at college by taking twice as many classes. In my effort to become a professional ballet dancer, I had been dancing six hours a day on top of that. My illness forced me to drop half my classes and give up my roles in the upcoming dance performances. I'd fallen into a deep depression, which made my illness worse. I could barely get out of bed. I had been sick all the time as a child and adolescent and was beginning to realize the doctors, diagnoses, and pharmaceuticals weren't helping me. I needed to make a radical shift. This trip to Hawaii, I figured, was either going to heal me or kill me. But some part of me knew if I could get myself to Oahu, the *mana* (land energy) of the island would bring me back to life. And yet here I was, drowning. The strength in my already-very-weak body was fading. I was going under. And my world suddenly went black.

Just then a man appeared. He was Hawaiian and wearing swim fins. He looked incredibly peaceful and calm. Dark hair, dark skin, beautiful smile, kind brown eyes. "I'll hold you," he said to me. "I'll hold on to you until the lifeguard comes." He reached for my arm to pull me close. Then, with gentle hands, he grabbed my hips and held my head above the water. He radiated serenity. A calm enveloped me.

And then the lifeguard appeared. He had a red flotation device tied to him. "Grab my wrist," he yelled as he extended his arm. It was difficult to hear him over the sound of the crashing waves. I grabbed his wrist, and he wrapped his hand around my wrist, holding me so tightly it hurt. "We have to take the shore-pound in," he yelled to me. "Do NOT let go of me! Hold your breath!" he screamed.

"Okay," I responded, too weak and limp and scared to say anything else.

"Now!" he yelled. I gulped in oxygen. And we went for it. He pulled me down and forward. The water caught us. We got lifted and slammed into the sand, and lifted and slammed again, and around and around and around we went, head over feet over head over feet. Underwater was dark and sandy and cold and heavy. My wrist ached from where he held me so tightly. I thought my bony wrist was going to snap. My lungs burned from needing to breathe. My back and neck cracked repeatedly as I was smashed in all directions.

And then we came up for air, in shallow water; my feet could touch the bottom. "Run, run, run!" he screamed as he ran alongside me, desperate to get us completely onto dry sand. The sand was deep and wet and made it hard to get a foothold. The water was still swirling around our thighs and lower legs. I used all the energy I had left and ran with him until he and I both collapsed in dry sand. We lay side by side, panting. And then I began sobbing. "It's okay," he said. "It's okay. You are safe." He held my hand and sat up. I kept crying.

Latham appeared and collapsed, panting and crying next to us. He had been running down the beach, a long run in very deep, soft sand. He had gotten his board to shore and turned around just in time to see me getting swept down the beach. He began screaming, and his screaming alerted the lifeguard and initiated the rescue. He had watched the whole thing, panicked, as he ran south down the beach.

"Where is the man?" I asked, dazed and confused.

No answer. Just labored catching of breath.

"Where is the man who was holding me?" I asked.

"What man?" the lifeguard responded.

"The Hawaiian man. The one with fins. The one who was helping me swim," I said. The lifeguard looked at Latham.

"There was no man," Latham said.

"Yes," I responded. "There was a Hawaiian man holding me afloat when you got to me. I let go of him to grab on to you."

The lifeguard looked out at the water and then back at me. "Renee, you were all alone."

CHAPTER 3

Opt-Outs

A woman I called who reads the Akashic Records told me something interesting. Fascinating, really. That we schedule "opt-outs" in our lives. That before we incarnate, our soul schedules moments in our lives where we can leave, instantly, if we no longer want to be here. These are the accidents that seemingly appear out of nowhere. They are the illnesses that turn overnight into death. They are the heart attacks and the strokes, the overdoses, and any other way the body chooses to shut down rapidly. Yes, our main exit may also happen in these ways; slow, drawn-out illness and deterioration are not a prerequisite to death. We may always choose, as Abraham-Hicks says, "Happy, healthy, happy, healthy, happy, healthy, dead."

I had called this woman the morning after I had a serious snowboarding accident. I had been racing down a mountain that was covered in eighteen inches of fresh snow, when I hit a buried boulder, flew into the air, landed on my head, but miraculously ducked my neck and rolled out of it. I ended up laughing hysterically. And by the time that evening came around, I was absolutely sure I wanted to completely change the life I was living: leave New York, quit school, get rid of my business, break up with my boyfriend, and move to Colorado to write. And I wanted to do it *immediately*. I didn't mention the snowboarding accident to her, but I did ask her why everything in my life shifted so quickly and I wanted such a radical change.

"Renee," she said. "Ski accidents happen all the time. And no one asks questions. Your soul had scheduled an 'opt-out,' but you decided to stay." Goose bumps ran up and down my body as I remembered ducking my neck and rolling. I could have just as easily broken my neck and died instantly. More goose bumps as I realized the last thing I did before I got on the plane was rewrite my will and have it notarized.

She told me that when we get to these points in our lives, we have a choice: to allow the transition to nonphysical, or to stay in physical form and continue, usually with a new appreciation of life and a lesser need to hang on to rigid, stale, limiting belief systems, to "shoulds." And almost always ready to make whatever major life changes are necessary in order to get on our True Path. Many times the body enters the coma phase, where the soul gets a chance to review the life so far and decide if it wants to return to the body or move on.

Death is not something we should fear. It is not the end. It is merely the dropping of the physical form and the transition back into Light, back into Pure Love. Have you ever watched a bug die, a pet, or anything/anyone for that matter? It is so *clear* when the spirit leaves. It is so clear that the physical form has been left in this realm and that the soul has moved on. It really is a miraculous event to witness. And, for those of us who can see, or feel, or hear nonphysical, we get to witness the departure and see, feel, or hear the *explosion* into freedom and joy.

It makes me sad that our culture, that many cultures, do not celebrate this transition, that we are not taught when we are children that this is an occasion for celebration, that the soul has accomplished what it was meant to accomplish on Earth and that it has graduated, so to speak. Or, in the case of an "opt-out," it has chosen to go rest, review all it has learned, and come back and try again. In the case of a beloved pet, it has endured as long as it can in the physical form and must return to nonphysical in order to switch out bodies. Animals are such pure beings that they cannot stay in this denser realm as long as humans can. They must return to nonphysical and regroup much more often than humans. But it only makes sense that they would switch out bodies and come back to us. The same with our human friends. Over and over. Lifetime after lifetime. Anything else would be too cruel. And, if we pay attention, we always recognize our beloveds when they return.

CHAPTER 4

PeLe

It had been ten years since my cat, Kai, made her transition to non-physical, and I suddenly felt ready to have her back. Impulsively, I went to the local animal shelter's website and clicked on "cats for adoption." There were ten. The first wasn't her. The second, nope. Third, no. Fourth, no. No, no, no, no, no—wait!

Puffy. A tabby Maine coon mix. Cat number ten.

Kai had been a calico Maine coon.

There she was! My baby girl.

My heart swelled with delight, and I recalled the last time we were reunited at an animal shelter in South Florida, when I was eighteen years old. I had been looking for a kitten and was happily playing with six of them, but a six-month-old calico Maine coon kept howling in her cage. Finally, I walked over to her, simply to comfort her, and she reached her paw through the cage and touched my arm. It melted my heart, so I opened her cage and she leaped into my arms, wrapped her paws around me, nuzzled her face into my neck, and purred so loudly I thought she would shatter her voice box. I took her home, and instantly she became the love of my life.

As soon as I saw Puffy, I closed my computer and grabbed my car keys. Kai-Puffy, here I come! I had the biggest smile on my face.

When I walked into the cat room at the shelter, many of the cats approached me. Some rubbed along my ankles. Others stood and looked at me, yelling their need for touch. I bent down and spent time with all of them. But I did not see Puffy. Extracting myself from all the furry love, I walked to the front desk. "Excuse me. I came to see Puffy. Is she here?" I was suddenly terrified someone had already adopted her. The man peered over into the cat room. "She's asleep in the cat bed on the counter. You can wake her up. Pick her up." He then turned back to his computer.

I went inside, eager to hold Puffy. Excited for her to recognize me the way she had in Florida. I gently stroked her, already completely in love, and then slid a hand under her tiny body. She felt much smaller than she looked in her photo. She had a lot of tangled, matted hair with a skinny body underneath. I began to lift her, and she hissed and spat and jumped out of my arms. She strutted across the cat room, hissing at every cat she passed, and made her way to a food dish.

Puffy's a bitch, I thought to myself. I stood there surprised. I had not expected her to react to me like that. I had imagined her recognizing me. I was so sure she was the reincarnation of Kai.

I looked at her a moment longer, and then the self-doubt drifted in. *I must have been wrong,* I thought. I gave her one last glance, but she kept her back to me, and then I left. I did not want any of the other cats; I wanted the reincarnation of Kai. A bit dumbfounded, I walked back to the parking lot and climbed into my car. *How could I have been so wrong?* I thought to myself. I gave up the notion of finding Kai. I didn't need a cat; I needed to heal. I drove out to California for a few weeks and tried to put the pieces of myself back together. I had been so shattered in New York.

Six months later, I was outside on a lounge chair when a cat appeared on my patio. I looked up, and she was just sitting there, on the upper level, staring at me. Her presence was majestic. She was regal. A goddess. She sauntered through the flowers and came to drink from my Buddha fountain. Then she turned around and stared at me again. A piercing gaze. Intense for such a tiny creature. Green eyes, full of fire, stillness, and ancient wisdom.

"You are *so* beautiful," I said to her. "What's your name?" (I noticed she didn't have a collar.) She held my gaze. "Pele" popped into my mind. (Pele is the Hawaiian goddess of fire, lightning, wind, volcanoes, and the creator of the Hawaiian Islands. She is beautiful, and she is fierce. It is said that when Pele appears, awakening is imminent.) There was no other name for this goddess kitty. Pele. She was definitely Pele.

"Hello, Pele," I said. "Thank you for coming to visit me. I love you." She walked over to me and jumped into my lap, then purred. Such a loud sound coming from such a little body. She gazed into my eyes, hers overflowing with love.

I gently began to stroke her, and she started to clean herself, as content in my lap as if she'd been with me for years. I marveled at how wonderful she felt, this minuscule furry warm body wriggling around on my lap as she stretched and twisted to get every part of her clean. Suddenly it began to rain. We both jumped up, and I invited her inside. She didn't follow me in, however. So I quickly made her a plate of tuna and showed it to her from just inside the door. She sniffed a bit, walked toward me, then entered my home and rolled around on my carpet, belly up in the air, purring.

Next she came over to the tuna and ate. She then hopped up on my sofa and spread out stately, like a queen observing her domain. I watched her in awe. She was so self-possessed. So graceful in her movements. She fit my house perfectly. My furnishings were gray with green accents, and the gray in her fur together with the green of her eyes made her blend in like she was born to live there.

After grooming her entire body, she began to explore my house. *Uh-oh,* I thought, *she is going to pee and poop all over. And spread fleas.* But I let her go. And she was the perfect guest. She inspected almost every square inch, but no pee and no poop. And no fleas. She stayed all afternoon, sleeping peacefully, curled up on my sofa, and at twilight she suddenly got up and left. "Please come back," I said to her as she walked out the door I had left cracked open since her arrival.

The next morning I sat on my patio, waiting. Quietly she appeared like a goddess from the bushes. When she saw me, she jumped up into my lap and purred. I told her how happy I was to see her and how much I had missed her. She gazed into my eyes lovingly and began her grooming routine. Eventually I went inside, and she followed. She stayed all day and into the evening. I drove to the store to buy a litter box, litter, and cat food. I left a window open so she could leave if she wanted to, but she was still there when I returned. As I got into bed that night, she crawled on top of me and purred on my chest. At one point I woke up to her sleeping on my pillow with her head on my face. *Isn't it a little soon to be sharing a pillow?* I thought to myself, wondering if wild cats had worms. And if cat worms could become people worms. But she was sleeping so soundly and her furry body so close to mine felt so comforting, I didn't move her. And all the time I left a window open, in case she wanted to leave.

The next day I text-messaged my brother with a photo of Pele and the words "Look! I found the reincarnation of Kai. She appeared on my patio!"

"That is your neighbor's cat," he responded. "You are a cat stealer."

This is so like my brother. Ignore the magic and miracles and go right to "the problem."

"It's a wild cat," I said.

"No, it's not. First, it's been shaved. Look at her coat. Second, you are surrounded by coyotes and foxes. That cat would not survive if it was wild," he wrote back.

I looked at Pele. Her coat had been shaved. It was obvious. And what remained was perfectly groomed. She was definitely not a wild cat. He was right. I was a cat stealer.

Reluctantly, I created a FOUND CAT sign with a photo and posted it outside our local grocery store.

A day went by and no one called to claim her.

A second day went by and no call.

I began to relax. *She* is *my cat,* I thought.

A third day went by and no call.

I went out and bought toys and more food and more litter and a bigger litter box.

A fourth day. No call.

She was my cat.

Every night she slept on my chest, purring. Every day she curled up in my lap, purring. When I would turn sideways at night, she would shift from lying on my chest to lying on my side and would wrap her paws around my arm and snuggle close. We were completely in love.

On day five my phone rang. I did not recognize the number.

"Hello," I answered.

"Yes, I'm calling about the cat. It is my wife's cat, Harry."

My heart sank. "Oh, but she is a girl cat," I responded.

"Yes, 'Harriett.' She has a lion cut and a broken tail tip."

He had described her well.

"Yes, that's her," I responded.

"Oh, my wife will be so relieved. Can she come get her now?"

"Yes, of course."

I gave him my address and directions. They lived close, about a ten-minute walk.

Ten minutes later my doorbell rang, and I opened the door to meet a beautiful older woman with piercing blue eyes.

"Hello, I'm Susan," she said. I liked her instantly.

"I'm Renee," I responded.

We shook hands.

"My pet psychic told me Hari was here. I was so worried she had been eaten or hit by a car, and the psychic told me she was in a very loving home nearby. That she was being well taken care of."

Pele had been outside and just then came in the patio door.

"Oh, Hari!" Susan exclaimed.

We both sat down on the steps in my front foyer.

"Come here." She held her arms out lovingly, tears of joy moistening her eyes.

Pele looked at her, then she looked at me, and then she walked over to me. She crawled into my lap and began to purr. I was embarrassed. Susan looked surprised.

"I have fallen in love with her," I said. Then I gently nudged Pele out of my lap and toward Susan.

She walked over to Susan and gave Susan some love. Then Susan picked her up to put her in the animal carrier she had brought. Pele extended her limbs, claws out, and began scratching and hissing. Susan used more force and got her into the bag.

"I'm not sure she wants to be with me," Susan said, confused.

Pele was howling from inside the bag.

"Maybe she just got used to being here," I said. "I'm sure she will be so happy once she gets home." I was trying to hold back the tears.

I gave Susan a hug and stood to open the front door.

As she walked out, I said, "Susan, if you ever need a cat sitter, please call me. I fell so in love with her while she was here." I felt as if my heart was breaking.

"I will," Susan replied. "And thank you so much for taking such great care of her. You may come visit her anytime."

I began to close the door.

Then I opened it. Susan was almost at the end of my walkway.

"Susan, how long have you had her?" I asked, though I wasn't sure why I was asking.

"Four months," she responded.

"And where did you get her?" I asked, again unsure why I wanted to know.

"At the animal shelter."

"Oh," I said. "I was there six months ago, and I don't remember a cat named Hari."

"Well, that's because we changed her name . . . Her name was Puffy."

Wait, what?

The lion cut. I hadn't recognized her!

My heart leaped, and I blurted out, "I went to the shelter six months ago specifically to *get* Puffy, and she hissed at me. She didn't want me . . ."

"Wow," Susan said. She seemed to let the reality, the synchronicities, sink in for a few seconds. Then she continued. "When my husband and I arrived at the shelter, she was sitting in the window looking out at the parking lot, and we knew she was ready to be adopted."

We both stood there in awkward silence for a spell.

"Well, it's nice to have met you. I'm glad she has a good home," I said. Susan was already down my driveway, holding howling Pele in a cat carrier, and I knew I had to let her go.

I closed the door and cried. I curled up on my sofa and sobbed. For ten minutes.

Then I got up and collected all of Pele's toys and litter box and food dishes and put them in the garage.

As I walked back inside the house, my phone rang.

I answered.

It was Susan.

"I don't think she wants to be here. She seems pissed."

I had no response. I wanted her back so badly.

Susan continued. "I am going to keep her in tonight because of the coyotes, but I will let her out again in the morning. If she comes back to you, she is your cat."

I exhaled a huge sigh of relief.

I knew she would come back.

The next morning I sat outside, waiting. She had been showing up almost exactly at 10:00 a.m. I checked my watch: 9:59.

And then from the bushes she appeared. Majestic. Holy.

She bounced down the steps, jumped into my arms, and purred her little heart out. And even though I always kept a window open for her, she never left again.

CHAPTER 5

ALEJANDRO

Argentina. Buenos Aires. A country known for wine, women, steak, and tango. It has been called the Paris of South America.

I dress the part. I live the part. I *am* tango when I am here. Feminine, sexy, lithe. My long blond hair is cut short and dyed dark. The cut is jagged, funky. I smooth it behind my ears. It shines black and ends just where my skull meets my neck.

Tonight I am going to one of my favorite milongas. The venue isn't beautiful, but the floor is smooth wood, the best dance floor of all—a huge improvement from dancing on the concrete, cracked tile, or warped wood floors of the other milongas—and because of this it draws the best dancers and the top DJs. From the street it looks like nothing, far from the city center, in a neglected neighborhood that is slowly becoming trendy. A nondescript door in a mean building, gray and crumbling on the outside. However, on Monday nights the door stands open, taxicabs idle in front, the drivers lean against the cars, smoking cigarettes. The plinks and plunks of tango music can be heard softly, coming from deep inside, as one walks by.

I saunter past the taxis and the smoking drivers and enter the tarnished, scratched glass and metal door. Continue down the long corridor lit by fluorescent overhead lights and lined with paintings and posters of tango dancers. A heavily made-up woman sits at a card table at the far end. She has a gray battered cash box in front of her and a wad of paper tickets. Strewn along the table are postcards and flyers for various tango clubs, dance teachers, shoes, and orchestras. Next to her is the door leading to the milonga. I pay my three hundred pesos (approximately three US dollars), get my tiny torn paper ticket, and go inside. The cigarette smoke hits me like a wall. My eyes and lungs take a few seconds to adjust. Most of the tables are already occupied and the dance floor is full; I have learned not to arrive before 1:00 a.m.; the *good* dancers rarely appear before then. The host spots me, comes close, and escorts me to a table for four that has a vacancy for one. He assures me I will be welcome there and leaves.

The room is square and not very large. Folding card tables, two deep, draped in cigarette-burned black tablecloths ring the dance floor; each has black metal folding chairs crammed around it, at all angles, many piled with tango shoe bags and jackets. A bar stands in the far corner. The walls are white, windowless, and hold large oil paintings of tango dancers on stretched canvas. No frames. The music is loud and the patrons talk over it. Dancers swirl around the dance floor. And harried waiters and waitresses, dressed in black pants, with white shirt and black vest, rush here and there, holding round black trays full of drinks. Wine, water, and Coca-Cola with Fernet are the drinks of choice. The most revered guests have champagne in buckets of ice on their tables, champagne flutes all around.

I take my seat and bend down to change my shoes, removing my heavy black orthopedic Dansko clogs and replacing them with my nearly weightless tango heels. As a foreigner, I am allowed to break the rules, or at least it's not as shocking when I do. No Argentine tango dancer would wear orthopedic clogs with a formal skirt, but I have learned how important proper walking shoes are, especially after a long night of dancing, and am not willing to sacrifice the integrity of my feet and legs in order to look sexy or elegant as I enter and leave a venue. I like to believe my dancing and my tango heels provide me with a type of we'll-forgive-the-style-breach credit. And I do notice the women look at me with awe and envy as I walk in and out of the milongas in comfort.

I fasten the tiny buckle on each shoe, arrange my toes so they are perfectly straight, tuck my clogs and tango shoe bag under the table, and sit up straight in my chair. As soon as I do, a man catches my eye. I hold his eye contact (which means *yes, I will dance with you*), and we get up from our seats and walk toward the dance floor. I have seen this man dance before, and I know he dances well.

We meet in the corner closest to my table, and he offers his left hand. I offer my right, and then I place my left hand on his right upper arm, just where his biceps meet his shoulder. As the woman, I get to choose how close I will allow him to hold me, what type of embrace: open or closed. And if I pick closed, I also get to choose how close. Because I am petite, I choose not to wrap my left arm up and around his neck; it would make my left shoulder lift too high and compromise my balance. Some men do not like this, taking it as a lack of desire to be close, or a fear. Some men interpret it as my not understanding close embrace.

But an advanced dancer (like the partner I am with) understands why I have chosen this embrace with him, does not attempt to move my arm (as some men do), and begins immediately to dance. Because of my shoe-changing, he had to wait a minute into the tango to get my attention, which caused us to step onto a dance floor with already dancing couples; and because of his knowledge of tango and etiquette on the dance floor, he has us moving out of the way of other couples immediately. I like this man, feel safe in his embrace, and close my eyes, as I do with all good partners. I get lost in the music, in how sensual it is—the violin, the piano, the bandonion, the singing, the lyrics, almost always about love and romance. I look for every opportunity I have to interpret the various sounds with my feet or my legs or an extra sway of my hips.

Argentine tango is a social dance, which means it is always an improvisation between two dancers. The man leads, and the woman follows; however, a good male leader will also follow the woman. It is amazingly intricate, difficult, and fun, each person never knowing what the next step will be or what the partner is planning. When both people know the music well, one can dance to the piano while the other dances to the violin, or any combination of the instruments or vocals.

I am consumed by the music, the movement, the interplay of our lead and follow, enjoying my time with this man completely, when suddenly I open my eyes and see Alejandro standing at the door. My Inner Guidance told me exactly where to look. I have noticed we can all feel when someone is watching us. Stare at someone in a restaurant or on a street, and that person will eventually look up and make eye contact. Animals will do the same thing. This proves, yet again, how protected we are when we pay attention.

Alejandro is watching me from the doorway. Athletic build, medium height, olive skin, huge black-brown eyes, and long dark curly hair. I have never seen him with long hair before, and it takes my breath away. He's dressed nicely, as I knew he would be; he's a traditionalist, even though he is so young for a tango master, and he honors the dance and the tradition by dressing formally when he dances, as do I.

His hands are covered with thick, chunky silver rings. He wears a wide leather bracelet on one wrist and some sort of leather and silver necklace; I can see it shining from beneath his slightly open shirt. A tango shoe bag is slung over one shoulder and across his chest. He smiles at me when he catches my eye. And my heart melts. His eyes are mischievous. I haven't seen him for close to two years.

A small crowd gathers around him. He is famous, after all. I close my eyes and continue my dance, knowing I will find him when the song ends. Knowing he is mine for the evening, knowing I have all the time in the world. An unspoken arrangement, but a good one. A solid one. We have wanted this for years, but circumstances have not allowed it. Tonight they will.

As I swirl in circles on the dance floor, in my partner's arms, I know how beautiful I look. I dressed carefully, as I always do when I go tango dancing. In my mind, getting ready is part of the event. And I relish applying my makeup and choosing clothing and matching shoes. As I have been shown by the masters: to dress with care is to honor the dance.

Tonight I have chosen a loose-flowing, knee-length black skirt and a tiny orange top. It is more accurately a piece of fabric with a string. The fabric, shaped like an oval, wraps behind my neck and drapes down over both breasts to gather just above my waist. A long string loops through the fabric under my breasts to cinch it tight and tie behind my back, like a bikini top would, leaving my entire back naked except for the string and the small, barely visible swatch behind my neck. I am wearing matching dainty, strappy orange-and-black high heels. The heel is impossibly thin, and four inches high. The straps are just wide enough to hold the sole to my size 6 feet. I feel his eyes on me as I dance away.

A few minutes later the song ends, I thank my partner, and from the far end of the room, I make my way across the clearing dance floor toward Alejandro. He notices me just as the next set of tangos begins and meets me on the dance floor. We smile at each other. Huge smiles. Our united hearts well up, traveling to move our lips into wide grins and exploding with love out our eyes as we gaze at each other. My body flushes with warmth. This type of connection, this type of electricity, is so rare. And we have felt it for each other for so long. To finally entertain the idea of seeing where it leads feels electrifying.

I wrap my arms around his neck. Press my body into his. Even in my four-inch heels, I stand on my tiptoes to reach him properly. I kiss him on the right cheek, and he kisses me on mine in response (the usual Argentine greeting). He wraps both arms around me for a moment, then raises his left, knowing etiquette dictates that we start to dance. In my heels and on my tiptoes, I *can* wrap my left arm around his neck without raising my shoulder, and to be this close to him feels like heaven.

He smells so good. Feels so good. I love it when a man smells like soap or cologne but so subtly that I notice it only when my lips and nose are against his skin. Anything more overpowers me and turns me off. Alejandro is a man who understands subtlety. His world revolves around it. He is by far one of the best tango dancers in the world, and what makes him so good—besides being panty-droppingly gorgeous—is how subtly he moves. How rarely he does the big flashy tango steps. How closely he holds his partner and how expertly he maneuvers her, how he shows *her* off and keeps his flash on the down-low, waiting for the opportune moment to throw in a wild move, just enough to show the audience he can, and then back to making it all about his woman. It works. Believe me. For the woman in his arms and for those watching. This man knows women, and he knows dance . . . and I get to be the lucky recipient of this knowledge tonight.

We begin to move. One body, four legs. He starts with just a movement of his rib cage that sends my right leg sideways to a ballet *tendu* (where the leg is extended along the floor until just the tip of the toe remains touching) perfectly timed to a loud bang of the bandonion. Another movement of his rib cage brings my leg back beneath me and, with a slight around-and-down movement of his torso, he wraps my leg around his to the sultry whine of the violin. As the space behind me empties, he moves forward into it, one large step, perfectly timed to the next *whomp* of the bandonion, and stops again, holding me tight and slightly rotating, allowing my free leg to interpret the sound of the piano with little taps of my toe and heel on the floor and against his feet.

In the past, even with this closeness, there was a distance between us. A respectful delineation of energy. He was taken. Or

I was. But now, tonight, there are no barriers. He is mine; I am his. The dance is completely different. I close my eyes, and I surrender to him, allowing him to lead me with his expert ability wherever he chooses. I can feel eyes on us. We are quite the coupling. With all my training, I dance quite well, and in his arms I look like one of the best in the world. Add to that the naked back, the tiny beautiful metallic high heels, and his long hair. My nails are short and painted Malbec red, my fingers covered with silver rings. His nails are trimmed beautifully, his fingers also covered in silver rings. From our hands to our formal clothing, to our shoes—his black patent leather and shined—we are the essence of tango incarnate.

A tango *tanda* (set) is four songs. It is customary to dance all four with the same partner. One song partially down, three to go. It was all happening too fast. It is also customary to chat a bit with one's partner between songs. This is left over from the time when children lived with parents (and had chaperones) until they got married; talking between songs on the dance floor was often the only time teenagers got to speak without being overheard.

Alejandro speaks first. "Estás hermosa." *You look beautiful.*

"Y vos tambien." *So do you,* I respond.

"I have missed you," he says.

"I have missed you, also."

He pulls me close, wraps his right arm tightly around me, and once again we begin to move.

This meeting in Buenos Aires is spur of the moment. I am dating an older man. Chris. A man who bought me in an auction. Okay, that sounds *way* worse than it is. I auctioned off tango lessons for a charity owned by surfers. They had a formal dinner and my dance partner, Joe, and I danced a tango: part entertainment and part auction item. A famous world-champion surfer bid for the lessons, but across the room a man kept countering, raising the price. When it got to $800, the surfer yielded, and the man across the room won. I met him at the end of the night. Handsome.

Strong. Athletic. A surfer. Clearly financially secure. And about fifteen years older than I was.

My father was fifteen years older than my mother, and they had been truly in love. I wondered if maybe this man was the answer to the hole in my heart, there since my father died. I was not in love with him. In fact, I was not in like with him. But I thought that maybe, because he checked off all the boxes (wealthy, kind, fit, athletic, handsome, surfer, smart, good job, huge house), I could fall in love with him, have some kids, be a trophy wife. The thing is: I didn't want kids. And I didn't want to be a trophy wife. And I didn't want to get married. But I was lost. I was thirty years old and still feeling lost. I had no idea what I was doing with my life, so I decided that maybe in order to be happy I needed to do what so many other women were doing. And I tried with Chris.

I didn't love sex with him. It wasn't terrible, but it wasn't great. I didn't love his company. And I didn't respect the way he spoke to his ex-wife or his daughter. These feelings I glossed over, however. Kept sleeping with him. Kept dating him. Until I received a phone call from my dramatic, endearingly funny, and wise childhood friend—Eric from Florida.

"How old is this guy?" he asks. Clearly smoking a cigarette and clearly holding the smoke in his lungs as he does, making his words come out stunted.

"Forty-five," I answer. He exhales as I respond.

Another drag from the cigarette. "And how much money does he have?" Stunted yet again, lungs filled with smoke.

"I don't know," I respond. Long exhale from Eric.

Third drag. "Well, Muffin, you better find out . . . Because what the fuck are you doing fucking an old guy if he doesn't have as much money as you do?" Eric says while exhaling, all in one long burst.

Oh my God, he was right! What was I doing? Why was I doing this?

With all that in mind, I went to Argentina. And happened to hear from Alejandro on the way. Who happened to also be flying to Buenos Aires at the same time. We planned to meet. In my heart I knew it was over with Chris; I would tell him when I got home. I just wanted the time away to be sure. Once Alejandro told me he'd be in Buenos Aires, I knew we would end up in bed together. It was long past time. Tonight was that night.

Alejandro did not sit with me; he was obligated to sit with the other masters. But each time I looked in his direction, he used his eyes and head nod, the *cabeceo*, to invite me to dance. I was pleasantly surprised. Surprised he wasn't dancing with all the top female dancers in the room. Surprised that he kept himself so available to dance with me. But he knew—and he is refined, and elegant, and a gentleman—he knew that if he was spending the whole night with me, it was his job to make me feel like the most important, most beautiful, most desirable woman there. And he said to me when I brought this up toward the end of the night, "I would have danced with you, and only you, all night, but I wanted to make sure the other men there knew you were and are available to dance with them." It endeared him to me more. If word got out that I was "his," out of respect for him, the men would no longer ask me to dance.

We left in the wee hours of the morning. Separately. Again, for my sake. So that I would appear single and would be asked to dance the rest of the time I was in Buenos Aires. I went outside five minutes after he did, walked around the corner, and discreetly got into his taxi. We went to my hotel, happily talking in Castellano the whole time. "A veces sonás exactamente como una Argentina," he said to me. "At times you sound just like an Argentine." We both smiled.

He carried my tango shoes in his left hand and put his right hand on my waist to escort me into the elevator. He pushed the button to select the floor and then the button to close the door. When the door closed, he immediately turned and kissed me.

Our first kiss, after all these years. His right hand on my waist, he leaned in and kissed me so tenderly, so sweetly. Just a baby kiss that lingered. Soft smooth lips. Kindness and love. And then a kiss on my neck, just above the fabric of my blouse, and another kiss closer to my ear. Not much time before the door opened.

When it did, he led me by the hand down the hall, fingers intertwined with mine, asked for my key, and opened the door. Once inside the room, he dropped the tango shoes, placed his hands on either side of my neck and face, and really kissed me. A kiss that lasted for a while. A kiss that tried to make up for wanting to do this for so many years and not being able to.

He untied my blouse. Easy to do. One pull of one string and it came undone. He slipped the fabric over my head. And took a moment just to look at me. "Estás hermosa," he said again. He pulled me in close, and we began kissing again. I started to unbutton his shirt. Both of us reeked of cigarette smoke. "Let's shower," I said to him. He smiled, kicked off his shoes, and began to unbutton his pants. I wanted to do that part, so I stopped him and took over, continuing to kiss him as I did so.

I had kicked off my Danskos the second we walked in the room, so the only thing left on me was my long black skirt and tiny little thong. I turned from him, leaving him in his socks and undies, and walked into the bathroom, turned on the water, removed my clothing, and got in. He followed me. Stepping in naked, and beautiful, and aroused.

He put soap in his hands and caressed me all over. Soft hands, slippery and wet. As he did so, he gazed at me as if I were the most beautiful creature he had ever seen in his life. Next he turned me around so my back was facing him, grabbed the shampoo bottle, and slowly and lovingly washed my hair. He moved closer and closer until he was pressed up behind me, body to body, kissing my neck, wet soapy hands caressing my breasts. I turned around, and we kissed again, me wanting to rush the shower, him wanting to prolong this stage as long as possible. Which he did. The shampooing and conditioning and soaping and massaging, hands and lips all over. Wet soapy body against wet soapy body, building the tension, savoring a time that can never be repeated. Like I said, this man was a master, and clearly not only at dancing tango.

We made our way to the bed. Alejandro was an excellent lover. He took his time. No rush at all. He delighted in every moment. He made me feel like the most desirable woman in the world. We fit together perfectly. And we fell asleep wrapped in each other's arms.

I woke up at some point shortly after, my soul smiling and supremely content, and I knew to the core of my being: I would rather be alone the rest of my life than lie in bed next to someone with whom I did not feel this type of chemistry. My heart swelled with gratitude for such perfect divine intervention, and I knew I had to break up with Chris the moment I got home.

PART 2

WILD RIDE

Life should not be a journey to the grave
with the intention of arriving safely in a pretty and
well preserved body, but rather to skid in broadside in a
cloud of smoke, thoroughly used up, totally worn out,
and loudly proclaiming "Wow! What a ride!"

—HUNTER S. THOMPSON

CHAPTER 6

BɘD BOYS

When we are not-whole, we attract into our lives not-whole people. When some part of us hates ourselves, we attract people who treat us badly. When some part of us wants to be saved by another, we attract broken people who also want to be saved, creating a codependent nightmare of wounds attracting wounds.

Only when we are truly ready to love ourselves will we allow into our lives good love. Until then, without realizing it, some part of us wants to be abused. Signs up for it. We want to be with people who do not treat us well; who love us and then push us away; who project their demons onto us; who are self-absorbed, self-obsessed, wounded, and abusive. People who are unable to offer anything besides broken, painful, intermittent love. Or people who are so needy they end up draining us emotionally, energetically, and financially. Either way, the result is shit. Sadness. Tears. Trauma. And heartbreak. With a lot of opportunity for growth thrown in, if we pay attention.

We deserve good love; we all know that on a soul level. But, because so many of us were raised in abusive or neglectful households, we feel bored by it, afraid of it, or unworthy of it. We are excited by the people who are damaged, the ones we are unsure of. We are thrilled by the danger of them. The "bad boy" or the "crazy slut." These are the people who turn us on, and we worry that if we were to settle with someone who is grounded and secure, we will be bored; that person will be boring. Or we worry that we will treat a person like that badly. Or we become obsessed with the idea of saving the damaged person, "healing" him with our love. We learned a broken love pattern as children; we learned that love meant kindness, cruelty, kindness, cruelty; and we crave that pattern of intermittent reinforcement—with the same fervor a gambling addict craves the intermittent reward of coins, chips, and cash. We lash out at people who love us consistently and unconditionally, subconsciously thinking something must be wrong with them to love us so much. We are afraid of being loved well because some unconscious part of us feels unlovable, undeserving. And so, until we uncover these traumas and break these self-destructive patterns, we push away content, thriving, secure people who are kind and emotionally available, and we attract in disasters who may seem exciting at first but end up treating us *terribly.*

In our soul's effort to heal, we attract people who say to us what a damaged part of ourselves truly believes. This is fascinating, when you think about it, because it means if we believe we are stupid, we will attract someone who tells us we are stupid; if we believe we are unattractive, we will attract someone who treats us as if we are unattractive; if we try to stay invisible, we attract someone who makes us feel invisible—so that we can see what is going on deep within. So that it comes to the surface to heal. So that we finally wake up one day and say, "No one gets to treat me this badly, no matter how much I love him. I have to love myself more. I can't tolerate this one moment longer." Then and only then do we finally say, *"Enough!"*

I spent thirty years of my life chasing the bad boys, going after love that didn't fit, that couldn't last, that wasn't love. Because my father—the love of my life—died suddenly when I was fifteen, a part of me was terrified of falling deeply in love and being abandoned. Without realizing it, in order to stay "safe," I chose guys who didn't fit me, ending up in relationships that could never last. Like I signed up in advance for something that would end, thinking that because I knew the end of the story, I wouldn't be shattered when it happened. Yet I was still devastated every time it didn't work out. Each breakup left me undone. Each breakup triggered fifteen-year-old-losing-Daddy wounds. But I never thought to stop the pattern, because back then I didn't understand it.

Only after my life exploded in New York and I was forced to do unfathomable cavernous healing work did I realize how deeply I didn't love myself. Before that it had never crossed my mind. But my mother's verbal abuse and neglect had caused me to hate myself the way she hated me—the way she hated herself—the way her mother hated her, the way her mother hated herself. So without realizing it, after my stage of choosing lovely men who would never last, I moved on to choosing abusive love. Not physically abusive, but emotionally abusive. I chose to be with men who used me, or men who were not honest, or men who wanted to control me. Yes, these men showed me the best of themselves in the beginning, but it wasn't sustainable.

Fortunately for me, most of them left me quickly. Subconsciously they knew that what they were presenting was a facade and that I would see through it eventually, so after a short period of intense and "perfect" romance, they disappeared, only to go find a new woman to whom they could show the facade until it faded and they had to move on to the next woman and the next.

In my phase of dating nice guys who wouldn't last, I ended each relationship—convincing myself something was wrong with each one of them. In my phase of dating assholes, they ended each relationship, and I convinced myself there was something wrong with *me*: that I wasn't young enough, or pretty enough, or sexy enough, or fun enough, or something enough. Never realizing that because I didn't truly believe in myself, because I didn't truly love and honor and respect myself, I kept attracting or choosing men who didn't truly love themselves, honor themselves, or believe in and respect themselves . . . and because their foundation was not solid, they did not have much to offer me. People can only love others as much as they love themselves. They can only treat others with the same amount of kindness with which they treat themselves. So while in the beginning everything appears perfect, most romantic relationships quickly disintegrate into power struggles because too many of us are entering into them *needing* something from the other.

Going after what doesn't fit us causes us so much pain. And hanging on when it's obviously time to let go causes more. Self-doubt causes us to cling. "Maybe if I tried harder," we say to ourselves. We stretch and stretch ourselves out of shape, compromising on what's important to us: *I guess I can put up with this. I guess I can put up with that.* Tiny step by tiny step, we betray ourselves in our effort to be loved, in our effort to be accepted. Telling ourselves, *This is marriage* or *All relationships are compromise* or *But he has so much good inside*; and in this betraying of ourselves, abandoning of ourselves, we become even more desperate to be loved by, and held by, and accepted by another, not realizing we have it backward. When we stop betraying ourselves in an effort to be loved, we will feel safe. The anxiety and fear will go. When we stop abandoning ourselves in order to please another, we will not "need" another to hold and love and protect us. We will finally be doing that for ourselves. And then, from this very safe and secure place of holding and loving and protecting our Inner Child, we will simply want the company of another. Not need it.

CHAPTER 7

ORPHAN

I'm twenty-nine years old, and my mother has just gone missing. I discover this when her best friend in Colorado calls me.

"Hi, Renee, this is Audrey. Have you heard from your mother lately?" she asks as soon as I answer the phone.

"No," I respond.

"I'm worried," she says. "She drove to Denver for a doctor's appointment a few days ago and asked me to watch Dennis. She was supposed to get back last night, and I never heard from her." Dennis was my mother's cat. "Every time I call her cell, it goes straight to voicemail."

I wasn't worried about my mother's cell going straight to voicemail. She was hopeless with that thing, and it was usually out of battery and lost under a seat in her car. I *was* worried about her not rushing home to her cat. She was obsessed with that cat.

I was at lunch with my brother and some friends. I hung up, told him, and immediately called my mother's assistant, who also had not heard from her in two days. The panic set in. But also the knowledge that if something terrible had happened, the police would have called us, wouldn't they?

My brother and I paid the bill, jumped in our cars, and headed north toward my mother's house and her assistant who was working there. Thirty minutes later, we arrived to the news that my mother had been found. Dead. In a morgue outside Denver.

Her body had been discovered in a bathtub in an AmeriSuites Hotel, drowned. The autopsy showed no foul play. The death was ruled an accident. How does a grown woman drown in a bathtub? So many questions, so much disbelief, so few answers. How quickly life just ends.

I am crushed. And lost. In shock. And an orphan. I can't sleep at night and can barely eat. The reality of having no one left to guide me, no more safety net if I fail in life, is almost too much to bear. Not having any idea how to process the loss or handle the radical change in my life, I decide to return to Buenos Aires, a place that has always brought me joy.

Tango empowers me. Tango uplifts me. The dance and the music fill my heart and heal my soul, so going back to Buenos Aires seems like the only thing I want to do. And, as broken souls desperate for healing do, I honor the call and go, renting a tiny apartment for two months and hoping that moment by moment, hour by hour, day by day I will surface back into the Light.

Still unable to eat well or sleep, I try natural sleeping pills that a doctor recommends. Not only do they not work, but they have the opposite effect: I am wired. Manic, wired, grief-stricken, afraid, depressed, malnourished, and sleep-deprived, I stumble around the city—not a very safe situation for any woman, let alone a shattered, recently orphaned twenty-nine-year-old.

In this otherworldly fog, I stand on the corner of the sidewalk, among a crowd of Argentines waiting to cross the street, my short, tiny body surrounded on all sides by taller people. The crowd moves a bit left, a bit right, a bit forward, a bit back as others join, waiting for the light to change, and I get jostled with it, wishing I had just stayed "home" and slept.

The day is hot. The air is humid. Diesel fumes, cigarette smoke, and street dirt fill my lungs. Car noises and Castellano chatter assault my ears. Horns, brakes screeching, cars accelerating. Gray storm clouds sit heavy in the sky above us, threatening to unleash a downpour of rain at any moment. Across the street the reds, blues, yellows, and purples of a gigantic mural beg for attention. Grime-covered trees wilt in the heat as they struggle to survive where they are planted in the concrete median.

The light changes and the people in front of me move, crossing the street. Women in swaying skirts, bare legs, and sneakers or sandals, cross-body bags slung over a shoulder. Men in tight shorts, T-shirts, and sneakers. Some in suits. Some alone, some in pairs and trios . . .

As I start to move, a wave of nausea and vertigo envelops me, so I hesitate a moment, seeking space from the departing crowd but erroneously using more time than I should if I want to cross the street before the light changes. I realize I need to hurry and take a step into the street.

As my foot leaves the curb, a hand pulls me back. It grabs the neck of my shirt and *yanks* me backward; the material of my shirt bunches up at my throat and hurts me as it digs in, choking me. At the same *exact* moment, my hair whips alongside my head and into my eyes because a *humungous* bus comes barreling by, *inches* from my face. It would have *killed* me. Instantly. Smashed the life out of my body right there.

The color drains from my face, my knees go weak, my heart starts to pound, and adrenaline surges through my veins, flushing heat to my extremities and causing me to tremble all over. I turn to thank whoever it was and find no one behind me. No one there. No one anywhere near. I am standing on the gray sidewalk completely alone.

CHAPTER 8

NO MORE BLAME

Why do we insist that we are all alone? Why do we insist that we are not protected? What is it about magic and miracles and divine intervention that turns so many people off? I cannot live without this truth. In fact, spending too much time with people who refuse to believe in magic and miracles and divine intervention makes me feel as if I cannot breathe. It's as if they come in with a vacuum and suck all the sparkles out of the air.

Because of this, I have spent almost my entire life searching for freedom. Trying to understand how to maintain a mind-state of bliss regardless of where or with whom I am. I got ordained as a Buddhist monk, was brainwashed in a Buddhist cult, burned everything I owned, alienated my family and everyone I loved, and stripped my life and my mind so bare that I almost didn't stay in my body on this planet. And what I have discovered is this: each of us gets stuck with the hell inside our own mind, and each one of us holds the key to liberation. Each of us holds the ability to turn our own hell into heaven. For me the key ingredients for heaven are love, gratitude, surrender, forgiveness, and faith.

The more we try to control the uncontrollable wildness of life, the more we plunge ourselves into hell. The more we look at people, places, things, and events and focus on what we dislike, the more we plunge ourselves into hell. The more we close down our hearts, refuse to forgive, and separate ourselves from others, the more hell we create. And the more we judge, the more we condemn, the more hell.

Because everything is a mix of "good" and "bad," everything is a mix of what we like and what we dislike. And as we focus on what we like in each person, in each event, in each circumstance, the more we draw that out and get to reap the benefits of it. The more we focus on what we dislike, the more of that we attract and the worse our experience gets. It takes constant vigilance of mind to catch ourselves when we are complaining, judging, or condemning, but it gets easier and easier the more we practice.

Life in a human body is messy. We live in a land of dichotomy. So we will always feel and experience the opposites. We are supposed to. And we need to if we want to have the fullest, richest experience here on Earth. In order to experience the highs, we have to know the lows. In order to understand pleasure, we have to live through pain. But where do we spend the majority of our time? Do we wallow in and indulge the negative states, or do we find ways to lift ourselves out of them? I have discovered that true joy is feeling gratitude for being alive even while stuck in a darker state of mind. In this way, happiness may be fleeting, but joy stays.

Happiness is wonderful *because* it is fleeting. We humans tend to not value as highly the things we are exposed to continuously. We value what is rare. We appreciate more what is ephemeral. And, if we are honest with ourselves, life without contrast would be extremely dull. Often we have our highest highs after our lowest lows. This is the roller coaster of life.

We are taught to believe we are supposed to be happy all the time. We are taught to value the positive emotions and to ignore or stuff down or quickly transcend the negative ones. Especially in spiritual communities. There is so much talk about "love and light," and yet, as humans, we will also experience anger, fear, depression, anxiety, and darkness. In fact, the more love and light we hold, the more darkness we will also hold, because "as above so below." The way we transcend these darker states of mind is that we marvel at them. As Kahlil Gibran says in his beautiful book *The Prophet*, "And could you keep your heart in wonder at the daily miracles of your life, your pain would not seem less wondrous than your joy."

As we gain wisdom, we learn to not act when we are in a fearful, depressed, anxious, or angry state of mind. That any action we initiate from this mind-state usually leads to results that are unfavorable. Because we are not seeing or thinking clearly. As we would wait, if we were walking a treacherous road, to take the next step until we could see, it is much better to wait out these darker states of mind, hunker down and remain still, trusting light will appear eventually, and then move when we can see again through a lens of love.

When we take responsibility for our own lives and our own safety, we get our power back. When we stop buying into fear-based narratives, we get our power back. When we take full accountability for all that happens to us, we stop being victims, we stop being broken, and we become whole.

There will always be something "out there" that will upset us. There will always be something to seethe against. But there is so much good. So much that we love. The youth glow with life force energy because they go with the flow and they focus on all they love. So many of the old get brittle and gray and dried up because they are fighting the flow of life, annoyed by everything, lobbying to create more and more rules in order to take the chaos that is life and corral it into something manageable and "safe" and predictable. Which is futile and literally drains the life force energy from their cells.

Freedom, I have discovered, is letting go and jumping into the stream of life. Being willing to be uncomfortable and trusting that divine choreography will always lead us to the next right unfolding. It is looking for the good in everything we gaze upon or stumble upon. It is, as *A Course in Miracles* states, finding the miracles in each moment instead of the grievances.

Freedom is letting go of blame and taking full responsibility for all that happens to oneself, even and especially childhood trauma. It is backing up enough to get the perspective to see that our soul chose our family and our childhood setting in order to experience certain things and learn certain skill sets to make our difference in the world. To live out our destiny. If that is not an empowering perspective, I don't know what is. By living through trauma, we become experts in that trauma, and when we overcome the trauma and thrive, we become experts in how to heal. Which then allows us to help others heal.

I parallel this to Special Forces soldiers. They sign up for hell in order to save people. They don't bitch and moan about it. They endure it. And then they sign up to work in hell. Simply to help liberate the oppressed. We can do this, too. As soon as we change our perspective from victim to warrior.

This change in perspective takes a person from curled up in a fetal position, helpless, hating the world, and waiting to be saved, to a full-blown empowered adult saying, "I chose that and now I rise—battle scars, war paint, stronger, tougher, fiercer, wiser—and now I go use all I have learned, all I have endured, to help others."

Kahlil Gibran also writes, "The deeper that sorrow carves into your being, the more joy you can contain." He explains with, "Is not the cup that holds your wine the very cup that was burned in the potter's oven? And is not the lute that soothes your spirits the very wood that was hollowed with knives?"

People get angry at me for suggesting that we chose the trauma we experienced. People cling to victimhood. And that is fine. It is a perfectly valid way to approach life. But there is no growth there. No power. No freedom. I know because I did this, too. My father's death traumatized me greatly. My mother was an emotionally abusive alcoholic who did not feed me when I was a child. She smashed a glass sculpture into my face when I was less than two years old, almost killing me and causing me to undergo weeks of reconstructive facial surgery. I should have been disfigured for life, but my body miraculously healed completely. While she tried her best and in many ways *was* wonderful to me, she scarred me deeply, leaving me incredibly insecure and constantly struggling with adult romantic relationships.

But I had this epiphany a few years ago on my book tour, when I got taken advantage of during a book signing by a woman who offered to "help" me when I didn't have the equipment to process credit cards and could only accept cash. She was also selling books for the author she represented and told me she would accept credit cards for me and write me a check for all my sales. My epiphany was this: Victim mentality creates a life of being taken advantage of.

When it came time to collect my earnings, she told me she charged 40 percent for helping me. "I always do a 40/60 split with my authors," she told me. I wasn't "her author," and this was something she should have mentioned before offering to help me. Next she conveniently got the sales count wrong, telling me I had sold fewer books than I had. I timidly stood there about to cry. I was caught so off guard, I didn't say anything. I just allowed her to rip me off, carried my remaining books to my car, sat in the driver's seat, and sobbed. *I just told the story of being broken to the point of suicide and scratching and clawing my way out. How could she do this to me?*

And then it hit me: I had spent thirty minutes talking to the group about being a victim: a victim of losing my parents when I was young, a victim of being abused by my mother, a victim of being brainwashed by the cult, a victim of being taken advantage of by the guy in New York, and a victim of being slandered in the New York tabloids. Guess what? She jumped right on that train and made me a victim, too. It was a powerful lesson, but I never told that "poor me" story again. I changed my entire presentation. From that day forward I began my talk with, "A lot happened to me, and for those of you who read my book, I am happy to answer any questions you have, but I'd like to focus this talk on the ways we triumph after tragedy and how we turn our pain to purpose . . ." I had never seen myself as a victim before I joined the cult. Since that undoing, without realizing it, I had somehow adopted a "poor me" persona. Which, I now realized with hindsight, had created a complete unraveling in my life.

I became *much* more powerful because of that woman. She gained about $75 and some really bad karma; I gained wisdom. I transformed myself in that parking lot. Like Superman going into a phone booth, I went into my car as Clark Kent. By the time I got out, my superpowers had begun to reappear.

CHAPTER 9

PRAGUE

I met him on the train from Vienna to Prague, a five-hour trip through vibrant yellow sunflower fields, rolling green hills, and beautiful countryside, interspersed with patches of small colorful buildings and sharp, pointy cathedrals. I had been in Europe for two months and was ready to go home, but my mother and her side of the family were Eastern European, and I felt a call to go there, so I bought a ticket and got on the train, picking two empty seats at the back of the compartment, facing forward. I slid over to the window seat for an unobstructed view.

"Is this seat taken?" he asked just as the train began to depart. "No," I responded, and moved my bag to the floor. He was younger than I was, just out of college, and nerdy. He had a kind, easy, naive energy about him. Young, mocha skinned, Indian heritage, living in the United States. He was eager to be traveling around Europe and excited to talk about it. We enjoyed getting to know each other on the ride, and by the time we arrived in Prague, at midnight, we had decided we would go look for a hostel together. Platonic. One room, two beds.

We both needed cash. Which is not the best situation to be in at midnight in the train station of a foreign country. From the train station we followed the signs to the subway, and in the stifling, underground heat and stillness of night, we found an ATM. He went first. Got his money. And put it in his wallet, which he then put in the small outside pocket of his backpack. *Dangerous,* I thought.

I pulled some money out of the machine, and while still facing it, took my backpack off my back and swung it around toward the ATM, but instead of putting my money in my pack, I carefully raised my shirt and put it in the money belt attached to my waist and nestled under my jeans, below my shirt, using my backpack and the ATM to shield what I was doing. I tucked it all away safely and then returned the backpack to my back. *Common sense,* I thought.

The subway station is hot and humid and dingy. It's painted off-white with random squares colored yellow, green, blue, and black. The lights are dim, and I find it slightly depressing. The train tires squeal and screech on the rails as the cars come through. Powerful. Metal. Clanking. Loud. While it's the middle of the night, there are enough people around for me not to feel afraid. He and I wait side by side for a train going to the center of the city.

When the train approaches, I scan the cars to see who is inside, as I always do with subway cars, so I do not enter one with people who make me nervous. The closest car has maybe five people, all of them older than we are, looking very tired: workers going home after a late shift. Some men, some women, all spaced apart as if they are traveling alone. The doors to the car open, and as we walk toward it, a group of three male teenagers rushes in ahead of us. *That was rude,* I think. There was no need to rush and push. We step into the car, but the kids will not move forward.

They stand just a foot and a half inside the door, side by side, and open maps. We say, "Excuse me," and nudge them slightly forward in our effort to get fully inside the car with our backpacks before the doors close. At the same time, people enter behind us and push us into the boys in front, who *still* refuse to move, holding their ground. Even though the subway car is mostly empty. It makes no sense. Why won't they move?

And then, as if of their own volition, both of my elbows shoot backward fast and hard. "Ooof!" I hear as both bony elbows, propelled by all the force my five-feet-three-inch body could muster, make contact with the people behind me. Knocking both of them out of the car. *We're being robbed!* The thought seems to come *after* my elbows move. All of it happening at lightning speed, my mind piecing it together: the boys in front, the maps, the refusing to move, the pushing from behind, my elbows moving. Just as the subway doors start to close and the three guys in front spin quickly and jump out. "Fuck!" my new traveling companion exclaims. His backpack has been slashed with a knife, and everything in that back outer pocket is gone. His passport, his wallet.

The people in the car are on their feet. All of them. Suddenly very awake and alert. "Stop the car!" they yell in Czech. One pulls on the emergency line. Nothing happens. We are plummeting forward into the darkness of tunnels underground at night. The gross fluorescent light in the car makes everyone appear like the walking dead. "This is why they won't let us into the EU!" a man exclaims in heavily accented English, enraged. "It's because of this shit!"

Then to us he says, "I am so sorry. I'm so sorry this happened to you. Is there anything I can do—we can do—to help?" I still have everything intact. Nothing is missing. My new travel partner is in shock, and angry, and yelling for people to stop the car. "It's too late," I say to him. "Those guys are long gone. I have money and a credit card. I'll pay for you tonight and go with you tomorrow to help you get a new credit card and passport. I'll help you cancel everything tonight."

It was a long night. We got little sleep. And I spent the next day helping him get back on his feet. "Get a money belt," I tell him. And I show him mine. I loan him cash, fully expecting to never see it again. But he sent me a check. And a really nice letter. We had parted ways the following day. I wasn't in the mood to babysit.

But I have to say, this was such a wonderful example of Inner Guidance. Of how protected I was. Of how quickly my mind added up the info in front of me: the three teenagers with maps open, refusing to move forward into a wide-open space, and the shoving and pushing from behind. If the car had been crowded, I may not have noticed. But the empty space made it not add up. And I'll always remember how quickly my body moved. My tiny little bony elbows jamming with all my force backward and up, as if in a past life I had studied this exact karate move. I hit two men bigger than I was square in the solar plexus with enough force to knock the breath out of them *and* knock them out of the subway car. That's pretty fucking cool.

I stood by a man in that subway car in Prague, and he was a victim while I was not. He was bigger than I was, stronger than I was, and male. And yet he got robbed while I did not. I'm not just making this vibrational shit up. It really is true.

True spiritual teachers tell us that only a part of our spirit incarnates in human form; the rest remains in nonphysical. It is constantly guiding us, looking out for us. I have read that the hairs on our body stay connected to our Source, and this is why they rise (goose bumps) when we see, hear, and read truth. Our body is so incredibly wise. It is *always* looking out for us, warning us, but we have to pay attention. We must learn to stop overriding it. Stop clogging it up and numbing it out by eating, drinking, and inhaling non-foods, toxins, and poisons. We must make it our best friend, not our enemy. We must learn to love this self-healing, divinely gifted, amphibious, *miraculous* machine. And we must learn to be more present. The more present we are in each moment, the more aware, the more tuned in, the more responsive. He didn't notice what was going on—I did. My Inner Guidance alerted me, and my body reacted. What a wonderful way to walk through life.

CHAPTER 10

Size and Sexuality

When does the war with our body stop? Seriously. Aren't we tired of it? I can tell you one thing for sure: the little child inside each of us is fed up with us criticizing her/him. Our body has to be fed up with us, as well. It works so hard for us. It carries our soul through this world. It makes life on Earth possible and *pleasurable*. And most of us spend way too much time hating it. Waging war against it. Depriving it of food or sleep or breaking it down to near ruin with exercise. We say horrible things to it, we think horrible things about it, we fill it with toxins, and then we wonder why it manifests illness and disease.

We are beings of light. We are not beings of disease. But we have got to learn to love, cherish, adore, nurture, and *admire* our miraculous bodies. It's not our fault, really. We have been brainwashed by the media to believe we are ugly so that we will buy their products. We have been brainwashed by Western medicine and Big Pharma to believe we cannot heal on our own so we will buy *their* products. And we have been brainwashed by organized religion to think using our bodies for pleasure is sinful, shameful, and dirty. No wonder we all have so many body issues.

I am *tired* of thinking I need to look different than I do in order to find love, find joy, be accepted. I'm tired of looking in mirrors or at crappy quality cell phone photos and thinking I'm ugly. Noticing my wrinkles. Picking apart my posture and my expression. I'm furious with the media and cultural norms for brainwashing us *all* to think we are ugly. And I'm pissed off at my Catholic upbringing for making me think my genitalia is shameful.

Our bodies are *miraculous* self-healing machines. Our genitalia are the parts of these bodies that create *new life*. There is nothing ugly, shameful, or wrong about *any* part of our bodies. We *chose* the body we are in for a reason. Designed it before we incarnated. It works its butt off for us, no pun intended, allowing us to work and play in this physical realm. And anything besides total respect, love, care, and admiration for this precious body of ours needs to go. Now.

We watch our cuts heal. We witness our bones grow back together. We have all experienced our body going from a ball of cells to fetus to infant to toddler to child to adolescent to full-blown adult. How did we ever buy into the paradigm that our body cannot rid itself of injury, illness, or disease? How did we allow ourselves to get trained into continuously complaining about our biggest, most important gift as humans? Can we please make a vow, now, to shift our body paradigms?

Those in full-figured bodies are in them for a reason. If the bone structure is large, the body is *meant* to carry more weight. Trying to make it smaller than it naturally gravitates to be is an *extreme* waste of energy. Energy that should be used for love, laughter, joy, and offering one's divine gifts to the world. Often those with larger bodies are highly sensitive beings, which means their energetic wingspan is *huge*. That means they brush up against *a lot* in life, and they need the larger body to ground them, to protect them. Their job here as highly sensitive beings is important. They have *huge* gifts to offer.

Ladies with a larger, more voluptuous body type: when you are spending all your creative and mental energy fighting with your body size and hating yourself for each thing you eat, you are *wasting* all of that light energy that you are meant to shove into this world through your creation and your joy. You are using it instead for self-hatred. You are missing the point.

Look at the full-figured women who have truly embraced their size. Aren't they *powerful*? Don't they seem unstoppable? And can't you see how much they light up the world? Wouldn't you rather be that than a size 8? Seriously! And you *can* be because you already *are*. All you have to do is enjoy moving through the world in a bigger body. That is it. The rest will come. Effortlessly, easily, once you stop the war inside you.

Ladies who have a smaller frame but have put on a lot of padding: Trust this padding. Embrace it. Your soul is going through a change and needs to feel protected. Once you relax and allow it, your soul can then feel safe, make the upgrades needed, and then drop the weight when the time is right. Effortlessly.

I met a new friend who hated going to the gym. She told me her boyfriend had bought her the membership so she would lose weight. She also told me he would poke her belly when they were watching TV and make comments about her eating habits. My heart grew sad when I heard this. The Light that flowed through this woman was pure grace. Of course she was in a larger body. I explained to her that she probably needed the weight to protect herself. She had been through a lot in life, much of it trauma in the hands of men. She had also birthed three children into this world. And she was an incredibly sensitive, highly evolved being.

I gently suggested she quit the gym and that she love her body, nurture it. And then listen to it if it called her to go for walks in nature or eat healthier foods. But love it just as much when it wanted comfort food and naps. I also quietly suggested she begin to give herself all she was looking for from this boyfriend: the love, the validation, the safety, the acceptance.

She quit the gym. She began walking in nature. She left the boyfriend. And she lost sixty pounds in a year. Effortlessly.

I seem to be able to offer this advice to others but still have a difficult time accepting some of it myself. I get hit with thought waves of *I'm old and ugly and undesirable and might as well give up now because I'm only getting older and uglier.* Um . . . in what universe is this an okay thing to think about myself? Oh, here on Earth. This seems to be the way we women talk to ourselves here on Earth. Tying so much of our self-worth into what we look like. What a waste of time! What a waste of life force energy!

Can we please stop this? Only with years do we gather wisdom. And only with wisdom can we heal, and I mean *truly heal*, the youth. This world needs elders. This world needs the healing tonic of feminine energy. And it really is only after we have lived the first half of life that we truly understand how to nurture, to hold, and to make space for others. Only when we are older in years are we able to really sit still and simply witness and love. It is no longer supposed to be about us when we hit a certain age. It is supposed to be about where and how we give back.

And again, a truly wise, truly whole, truly content older woman radiates a sense of beauty, Light, love, nurturing, calm, and Divine Feminine energy that no younger woman can. If this is not attractive, I don't know what is. Think of your favorite grandmother or elderly woman. Think of the way you felt in her presence. Think of the soothing she brought to you. Don't you want to be like her one day? And again, you can be—we can be—because we already *are*. It is imprinted in each one of us to happen naturally as we age, if we stop fighting the process. Don't we want it to be said about us after we die, "I always felt better around her. I always felt peaceful. I always felt seen. I always felt safe. I always felt heard. I always felt loved"? Isn't that so much better than "She had a nice ass and tits"?

And speaking of ass and tits . . .

After shutting down my sexuality for close to seven years in the cult and five years after, I have realized it is *vitally* important that we let our sexual energy run freely. Just the word "vital" implies life force energy. We create life within our wombs. We birth it into the world. The shaming of and shutting down of women's sexual energy is causing a lot of the sickness on this planet. It's amazing to me how women shame other women for being sexually free. My mother used to yell at me to "close my legs" when she saw me stretching to practice for ballet class. My spiritual teacher said I was "blowing energy out my pussy" and that I "used my pussy to pull [her] man off the spiritual path." A woman who lives in my small town recently texted me and said if I would "open my eyes and close my legs" I would remember some event that never happened. How is it that we women have learned to shame other women in this way? And what about men using slang terms for female genitalia to insult other men? Women do the same to insult men. How has this become okay? I read a meme recently that said, "Why do 'balls' equate to toughness and 'pussy' equates to weakness when even the slightest flick to the nuts sends a guy to his knees and vaginas push out an entire human being?" I love this so much! In order to truly honor the Divine Feminine, our language needs to change.

By buying into the paradigm that women's sexuality is bad and dirty and shameful, we manifest sexual disease and we get confused about what's "appropriate." If passion is running through us, if the desire is there to merge with another—to be as close as two bodies can be together because the attraction is so strong—we should follow it. Bonding with other humans in this way is not bad; it's beautiful.

The second chakra, the chakra of our genitalia, is the generative chakra. It creates more of what is. When two humans come together and unite these parts of their bodies, they create another human. When two humans come together and unite these parts of their bodies to share love and healing, they create more love and healing on this planet.

There is mythology about the Venus temples. It is said that warriors who came off the battlefield would stop at the Venus temples before they returned to their villages. The women of the Venus temples understood that these warriors needed to lie with women, to make love to them, to be saturated in the energy of the Divine Feminine in order to be cleansed of the horrors of war. In order to remember love and truth, kindness and goodness, gentleness and healing, so that their closed-off, hardened hearts would soften and reopen, so that the soldiers would not bring the emotional and psychological sickness of war with them back to their villages.

Dr. Martin Luther King Jr. said, "Darkness cannot drive out darkness; only light can do that. Hate cannot drive out hate; only love can do that." The women of the Venus temples and the warriors who visited them knew this.

There is confusion in spiritual communities that sexuality is not spiritual. And this is simply not true. The more aligned a person is with Source, the more whole a person is, the more she or he is thriving. So the more Light is flowing through that person. Which means the more attractive that person is. Magnetic. And with this type of magnetism comes sexual attraction. We should not be shamed for this or try to turn down this Light. Any time we turn down our Light, for any reason, we make this planet dimmer. I am not saying we have to strut our stuff around half-naked, turning heads. I'm simply saying we need to be aware that we are sensual beings, sexual beings, and to shy away from these impulses because of shame does ourselves and the world at large an incredible disservice.

CHAPTER 11

ANYThiNG IS POSSIBLE

week after the 9/11 attacks I woke up to a strange phone call from my mother. She sounded like she had marbles in her mouth. And as she slurred and stumbled through hard-to-decipher speech, I pieced together the very sobering fact that she had had a massive stroke.

It took years for her to recover, but recover she did. I had flown to Colorado to be with her the day of that call, and the first doctor I met told me, while making zero eye contact and scanning her notes, that my mother would never talk, walk, or live alone again. She said my mother would be wheelchair bound and living in assisted living. Then she closed her clipboard and walked away. Leaving me in shock and utter despair. A second doctor, noticing my distress, sat me down in his office, held my eye contact, and told me it was impossible to tell what her end result would be until the brain swelling went down. He pulled up and showed me a scan of her brain. He suggested I get her to the best stroke-rehab facility possible and that I never stop believing in miracles. "Anything is possible," he said to me.

My mother ended up not only talking and walking again, but skiing, driving, and living on her own. However, she was changed. But changed in miraculous ways. She had always been stubborn and rigid and distracted and self-righteous and mean and critical and obsessed with her looks and social status. She used to barely ever hug me, and when she did, she held herself stiff, like a board. After the stroke, she would hug me and melt into my arms. She would leave the house looking like she pulled dirty clothes out of her hamper and say things like, "Oh, who cares what I look like? I'm just going to the store." She stopped going to church and would comment, "I love finding God in nature." And while my brother and I loved this new, softer, more authentic, much more lovable version of her, we hesitated to let her live alone. She often left stove burners on, overflowed the bathtub, or cooked meat still wrapped in plastic. I was living in California at the time, and my brother was getting burned out living with my mother in Florida. We needed to figure out a plan.

And then I woke up one day and could not walk. My hip felt like a sliding glass door that had fallen off the track. I went to doctor after doctor, and each one said the same thing: "You will never dance again. You will be lucky to walk without pain." They could not locate the source of the problem, but they all agreed I would never heal. The only solution was cortisone injections, but I did not want to do that. I had heard those injections were more destructive over the long term and that they masked pain, allowing the patient to injure the body more. I was devastated. My career as a professional dancer was over. And I decided it was time to move to Florida and help my mother.

Which I did. I packed up my life and drove to Florida. I ended up going to the joint specialists for the Miami Dolphins, and they put me in a CT scan machine and injected the sheath of my iliopsoas with cortisone. It hurt like hell, but it did help. A lot. I just knew I never wanted to do it again. So I made one more appointment with a doctor my professional dancer friends recommended. The appointment was months out; he was a very well-known physician and was fully booked. And until then I did the best I could to manage the pain.

The day of my appointment was the day I found out my mother had died, after she had gone missing. I was devastated and could barely breathe. But I had waited so long for this appointment; I had to go.

I arrived late. And the doctor was an asshole. "You are late," he said when I walked into the office, "and you are wasting my time." Tears welled up in my eyes and I choked out an "I'm so sorry."

I thought he would ask about my injury, but he did not. He simply made me stand in front of him, and he squatted down near the ground, examining my feet and ankles, then my legs, and eventually my hips, torso, neck, and head. I was barefoot, wearing short shorts and a tank top, so that he could see me well.

"You injured your fibula. It did not heal well. It's been throwing off your hips for years. It's no wonder your hip finally gave out," he said.

Wow! This guy was good. I *had* fractured my fibula in college. And because I had not wanted to lose my role in the dance performance that year, I'd kept dancing on it. Until it almost broke clean in half and I had to stop.

I started to talk, and he stopped me. "I could operate," he said. "I could charge you a ton of money and I could cut you apart. But I want to do this . . ."

He asked me to lie down on the examining table. "Close your eyes and picture your injury," he said to me. "What color is it?" he asked.

My mind flashed back to an elderly Vietnamese dermatologist I used to go to in Florida for acne. After I began studying massage therapy in Hawaii, I developed ganglion cysts in both wrists. When I asked him about them after he examined them, he said to me, "I could operate and remove them, but they will come back. I want you to try to heal them yourself. You can make them go away. Your body can dissolve them." I remember looking up at him in surprise. This was before I had read so many books on how the soul manifests disease or injury in the body in order to wake us up to something we are not seeing. But I thought about his words on the plane and I realized when I went back to Hawaii that my body was too small and energetically sensitive for me to be a massage therapist, and that all the massages I was giving were ruining my wrists; I would have to find a different career. I quit massage therapy and the cysts went away. They never returned. I became a surf model and professional dancer instead. The cysts saved me from a career choice I didn't love, and pushed me in the direction of careers I *did* love.

I was amazed this traditional doctor seemed to be suggesting a similar path to healing.

My mind returned to the site of my injury.

"Black," I said timidly. I could see black gunk, like tar, when I "looked" at my right hip.

"Ask it why you have it," he said. "Ask the injury, 'Why do I have you?'"

I began to ask and immediately knew the answer. I started to cry.

He allowed me to cry. He didn't interrupt. And then his manner grew softer. He asked, "Do you know why? Would you like to share it with me?"

I said, "To be with my mother. I have this injury so that I would move home to Florida and be with my mother."

"Do you need it anymore?" he asked me.

I began to cry harder.

No, I did not need it anymore.

"No," I said. "She just died. I found out today . . ."

His energy changed completely.

"Is this why you were late?" he asked me.

"Yes," I responded.

"Why didn't you say something?" he asked.

"I'm not sure," I said.

"I wish you had told me" was his response. No apology for his gruff greeting.

"Okay, now that you no longer need this injury, I want you to thank it and let it go."

I pictured the dark energy in my hip. I said, "Thank you" to it inside my mind. I began to cry again. Because of this injury, I had spent my mother's last months on Earth with her. I never would have done that. I had often hated living with her. I had left twelve years prior. If my hip hadn't stopped working, I never would have moved home. I thanked my injury again. From the bottom of my heart and from the depths of my soul. And then I told it I no longer needed it, that it had done a wonderful job, and that it could go.

"Have you thanked it and let it go?" he asked me.

"Yes," I responded. Sniffling.

"Okay, what color is it now?" he asked.

I looked with my mind. I saw the dark black tar-like stagnation go and be replaced with vibrant gold and turquoise energy. As I continued to "watch," I saw the gold and turquoise get brighter and brighter. "Gold and turquoise," I told him. It was shining with Light and was crystal Bahamian-shallow-water-over-white-sandbar blue.

"Good," he said. "You may open your eyes and sit up."

I did.

His whole face had changed. He looked so much kinder. "Your hip will heal now," he said to me. "It is healed. When people ask you about it, you say, 'I'm better.' And you believe it." He did not charge me for the appointment, and he apologized for his rough beginning.

The pain was noticeably less. It felt as if I floated out of there. The pain did not go away completely that day. It diminished gradually over weeks. Until I forgot I was injured. And then one day I noticed I was, indeed, completely healed.

CHAPTER 12

Mystic

When I was twenty-two years old I had sex with a guy I picked up hitchhiking on the North Shore of Oahu. He gave me genital warts. Turns out he was the local crystal meth dealer and an addict. I had to be drunk to have sex with him because every instinct in my body told me that union was not safe. I even went to the gross drug house he lived in with his drug-addicted mother. I had sex with him there on a disgusting, bare, filthy, stained mattress. I'm surprised I didn't get lice, or crabs, or fleas. Or leprosy.

I'm not sure what I was thinking. I suppose I was going out of my way to explore being the opposite of how my mother raised me. She seemed so shut down sexually. So reserved. So Catholic. So consumed with "being a lady."

One of the first classes I took in college was Human Sexuality. It was taught by a woman in her fifties, and on the first day of class she told us that a large percentage of women have never had an orgasm. I, myself, at seventeen years old, had never had an orgasm, and I vowed to myself, in that class, that I was not going to be one of those women. I went back to my dorm room that afternoon, locked the door, and figured out how to give myself an orgasm. And then I met Lisa.

She was younger than I was and the summer girlfriend of my college roommate. She was a beautiful young woman and an *exquisite* ballet dancer. And she was promiscuous. She seemed so free with her body. So comfortable. So at ease. She oozed sexuality and did not apologize for it at all. She wore tight, tiny outfits and bragged in detail about her sexual encounters. Her big blue eyes twinkled with light and mischief, her thick blond hair cascading down her back like a golden waterfall. I wanted to be like her. And, without realizing it, I adopted her persona.

It's a shame that organized religion teaches us that the most miraculous parts of our bodies are shameful. I understand why they do it: when we have sexual intercourse with another, especially when it is a celebration of love and a desire to be as close as two physical bodies can be with each other, there is a union with God. The love, the desire, the joining, the pleasure . . . it is all God. If we can do this with each other, we do not need the church. The church gets fewer followers, less money, holds less power if we can find God on our own. And this, making love, is one of the ways we can.

After my father died, I felt like a caged animal. I felt locked inside my mother's Catholic, uptight, rigid, you-have-to-be-a-lady, and women-have-sex-only-to-please-men paradigm. I was trying to understand where I fit in the world. And I was looking for intimacy. But once I discovered how fun and free it felt to merge with men in sexual intercourse, I dropped all my boundaries. As the extremist that I am, my pendulum swung from one side (prude) to the polar opposite (promiscuous). And for a while in my twenties and early thirties, I had sex with every guy I found attractive.

I'm not sure what I was doing, what I was trying to prove. I know wanting them to like me was in there. I know wanting to be the opposite of what my mother tried to instill in me was in there. I also think I was trying to squash the side of me that was extra-sensitive and spiritual; the side of me that remembered being a Light Being and was wondering what the hell I was doing on Earth was in there, too.

It's interesting to write this because, as I do, I realize that in my promiscuity I was trying to squash the spiritual me. And in my quest for enlightenment, I tried to kill the wild, untamed, human me. And in doing these things, I have felt split my whole life. The spiritual side of me is calm and patient. She is wise and knowing. She trusts divine choreography, and she is kind, incredibly kind. She sees the divine version of everyone and loves them all. But she also shies away from the world. She closes down. She gets overwhelmed by too much socializing, and she overanalyzes each decision, always checking in to see if it is in her highest good.

She basically closes doors to life. She withdraws. She retreats. And in her doing so, she gets depressed and does not want to be here. In her desire to have everything clean and everything neat and to not make decisions that pull her mind off-balance, she creates such a sterile world. (Go to bed at 9:00 p.m. so I can wake up at sunrise. Only one cup of coffee because otherwise I get jittery and can't sleep well at night. Exercise daily. Don't even think about dating because only one guy is the right guy, and he has not appeared yet. Be careful with sugar because it makes me have less energy . . .) Boring, boring, boring, boring, *boring*! Why even be here?

The other side of me wants to get drunk and screw the next hot guy who crosses my path. She doesn't care if he fits her economically or politically or in any other way besides being kind and sexually attractive. She doesn't care if she sees him for one night or for years. She wants to make a mess of her life. She wants to rattle the cage. She wants to sleep too late and drink too much and have so much caffeine she can't sleep and her body shakes. And in her doing so, she opens to life again. She says yes, yes, yes instead of no, no, no, no, no. And I believe, in this saying yes, the universe smiles. Because now the universe can offer her gifts in each moment. It's like going to a restaurant and saying, "I'll try everything on the menu," rather than going in and saying, "I can only eat vegetables with no sauce, and please don't give me carrots."

Back then I *was* reckless. I was wild. I was exploring who I was. Determined to shatter all the rigid paradigms of how the world works and what is "safe." Almost all the people who had been teaching me how to be in the world, what the world was like, seemed dead inside. Dried up. Bored, depressed, lifeless, lost. As soon as I realized there *were* other, more alive ways to be, I negated everything I had learned. I wanted to see for myself. I guess that's what a true mystic is: someone who does not take another's word for it, but instead chooses to find out herself.

Eventually I learned that sex without love was not fulfilling. In fact, I learned that sex without love often left me feeling emptier after. More alone. More lost.

When I was in the cult and after, I swung in the opposite direction: total celibacy for five years. I think this was worse than serial loveless sex. Not being touched, not being naked with another, not expressing such a passionate and feminine part of myself, shutting down all that energy . . . It was actually more harmful for my spirit, for my body, and for my expression as a woman.

Attraction is not up to us; we have zero control over who we are attracted to. People light up to us for a reason; it is up to us to explore the attraction in order to discover the reason. Sometimes there is only supposed to be friendship there, platonic. Often it is a reunion with a loved one from a past life. Sometimes it is a reunion with a nemesis from a past life. We must trust our Inner Guidance as we explore the connection. But when we shun it, turn away from it, close the door to it just because of preconceived notions, it becomes an important soul-growth opportunity missed.

I didn't need to be sleeping with every hot guy that crossed my path. That was rash. But it did serve a purpose. It taught me a lot about myself, about what I wanted, about true intimacy. It taught me that I could feel more alone lying next to another than I do when I am solo, and it taught me that I would rather be alone the rest of my life than feel forced to make love to someone I did not want to, just because of a commitment. I witnessed these types of relationships and marriages, and I knew they were not for me.

So many experiences are missed when we make up our minds ahead of time and don't experience the new because of fear. So many opportunities wasted. I don't want to be this woman anymore. I don't want to be the woman who screws meth-addict hitchhikers, but there has to be a happy medium, don't you think?

The genital warts went away, thank God. No trace of it in my bloodstream a few years later. And the experience served the larger purpose of scaring me and making me much more careful sexually.

But isn't this the million-dollar question? How does one combine all sides? All parts? All desires? How does one stay open to life and also honor true personal preferences? And how much self-discipline is the right amount? Does it come down to boundaries? Getting rid of "should"? Does it come down to a moment-by-moment decision? I want to be free again. I want to say yes to life more. And yet I'm not sure getting naked with the twenty-four-year-old tennis player and his best friend, the gift from the Book Tour Gods, was truly what my soul craved.

CHAPTER 13

Maldives

It's 3:00 a.m. I sleepily gather my backpack from the overhead compartment. I have been traveling for close to forty-eight hours straight, crammed into the cheap seats at the back of massively large planes. I feel disoriented. I feel dizzy. And as I stand, a wave of exhaustion hits, and the world spins for a second. I hold on to the seat next to me to keep my balance. Then I shuffle forward with the other passengers into the unknown.

I have just landed in Malé, the capital of the Maldives. The plan was to meet friends of mine here. Actually, to reunite with them at the airport in Singapore and fly together from there. Destination: Kanuoiy Huraa Island, North Malé Atoll. But that plan went to shit the moment Vanessa got a pre-travel physical exam and discovered she had breast cancer. So, here I am: travel weary; upset about my friend's diagnosis; in a tiny, sticky, cramped, dilapidated building; and completely unsure of where to go next.

I follow the crowd through the bright lights of customs and end up outside, near the water, in the hot, humid, heavy, gray-black obscurity of 3:00 a.m. Even with the noise of the early-morning greeters and taxi drivers, I can hear the tide lapping against the seawall and the small boats knocking against the dock. I smell the distinct odor of low tide and diesel.

A tall and thin middle-aged dark man in faded jeans and an old T-shirt is quietly standing away from the crowd. His black hair is long, thick, and shiny, and his face is serene. He holds a handmade sign that says RENEE. I approach him, and as I get closer, he holds his sign a little higher.

"I am Renee," I say.

"*Assalamu Alaikum,*" he greets me, with a slight blow of his head.

"*Wa-Alaikum-as-salam,*" I respond, not even knowing how or why I know what to say. I must have heard it on the plane.

"Peace be upon you" was the greeting. "And onto you peace" was my response.

He loves it and smiles. A big, bright, warm, welcoming smile. He puts one hand to his heart, bows slightly, then motions for me to hand him my backpack. I turn and point to my surfboard bag, which I had left just outside the exit door. I am traveling with a nine-foot-six-inch longboard, and the board and bag together, at 3:00 a.m., after traveling for forty-eight hours, feels too heavy for me to carry. He smiles again and walks over to it, hoists it onto his head, and then begins to walk toward the dock. I follow.

The dock is small and holds various open wooden boats. He approaches the closest, steps down into it, heaves my board bag in (it sticks out over the bow), motions for me to hand him my backpack, drops that into the boat, and then says to me, "Please," as he gestures to the tiny, rickety, splintered wooden vessel below us. My luggage and his weight alone make the boat appear as if it is going to sink. The dark, oily water is just inches below the railings.

I have a choice to make: trust that I will be protected and get in this boat with this strange man to venture off into the darkness, or walk back to that tiny airport and wait for a flight back to the United States. I get still. Check in with my heart. My intuition tells me I'm safe, so I get in the boat. And we set off, just the two of us, into the inky black, dead-calm sea, away from land, away from lights, and into the abyss of the unknown.

I ask him how long the journey will take, but he does not understand me. He simply smiles and replies, "Please." As we get farther from the airport, with no other land in sight, I begin to have doubts. *Please let me be safe,* I pray. *Please, God, please let me be safe.* We continue on in silence, across the dark ocean . . . ten minutes, fifteen . . . with my mind using my last reserves of energy to squelch any rising thoughts of doubt and fear. The small engine makes a whirring noise. There is only a slight breeze, created by our slow movement across the sea. And the stars appear brighter and brighter as we leave behind the glow from land.

At one point he stands up, leans forward as if looking for something. A tiny light appears in the far distance. He sets our course for this light, and I sigh with relief. Soon a small atoll appears. A tiny hut, illuminated from within, becomes visible. As we get closer, I see dark humps around the outside edges—bungalows, with what appears to be an office or main house, the one with the lights. Next I notice a lone figure on the beach.

My driver slows as we approach. He runs the boat directly onto the sand, very close to the silhouetted man, and as he cuts the engine, I am greeted by a hearty booming Australian accent. "Hello, Renee! I'm Tony! Welcome to Pasta Point!"

I like this man immediately. His voice is full of joy, good humor, and love. Tingles run up my skin, goose bumps—a sign of truth and goodness from Source. He reaches his hand out to steady the boat and to grab my backpack as the driver hands it over. Once he has my pack on his back, he holds out his hand to steady me, and I jump the five feet from the bow of the boat to the wet sand below. My knees buckle slightly from impact and exhaustion as I land.

"Amir will bring your board bag," he says to me. "You must be *knackered.*"

I nod.

"I need you to sign a few documents in the office, and then I will show you to your room."

He welcomes me into his tiny office and hands me a plate with a grilled cheese sandwich and a bottle of water.

"Renee, have a toasty." I love this man even more.

I sign the documents, hand Tony my credit card and passport to keep in his safe, devour the sandwich, and then I follow him to my room.

We walk along a narrow sand path, lined with old, faded bits of coral and conch shells, to a small wooden hut near the very edge of the rocky, sandy atoll. There are boulders around the edge of the hut, protecting the bottom of it from the waves lapping along the shore. He opens the creaky wooden door, and I peer inside.

My heart sinks a bit. From the doorway I can see two soggy twin mattresses on flimsy wooden slats, separated by a teetering wooden nightstand that holds a derelict lamp. We take a few steps inside, and I notice a wobbly wooden chest of drawers squished precariously in the corner behind the door. The mattresses are thin; the frames are frugal. Both beds are made with a set of stained, threadbare sheets and a lumpy, moldy-looking pillow. My surfboard bag and backpack are already inside the room, taking up all the space on the far side of the second bed.

There is an old ceiling fan spinning lazily overhead and a cutout hole for a window. No screen across it, just a small wooden slab held up by a hook; I suppose it ensures the window can be closed in a storm. The floor is old cracked tile; the walls are wood, both bare. The bathroom has a step down from the main room into a small puke-green tiled space that holds a water-stained toilet with no lid, a sink with one rusty faucet and two rusty handles, a pipe that protrudes from the wall next to the toilet with a metal control for water, and a bare bulb on the ceiling, with a long, dangling, filthy string for someone my height to reach.

"No warm water, I'm afraid," Tony says. "But it's so hot here, you won't need it," he adds.

"Please sleep well, and let me know if you need anything at all. My home is your home." He hands me the key to my room and walks out, closing the door behind him.

I feel homesick and alone. I am overtired, and I had been expecting to stay in something a bit more comfortable, with friends of mine in the cabin next door. I am scheduled to stay two weeks, and the idea of two weeks on these bedbug-ridden-looking mattresses makes me sad. It is so hot and humid in the room, I feel like I can't breathe. And with Tony not in there talking, I can hear mosquitoes buzzing around.

I want to go home, I think to myself. *This was a mistake; I shouldn't have come alone.* I sigh. I begin to cry. I'm so, so, so tired. *Take a shower and go to bed. You can fly home tomorrow,* I answer myself. Then I pull a beach towel from my board bag, some soap and my toothbrush from my backpack, undress, and walk into the sketchy bathroom.

I decide to use bottled water to brush my teeth, rinse my mouth and toothbrush with the same, and then turn on the shower and will myself under the cold water that comes pouring out of the pipe. *Fuck, that's cold,* I think. *I can't handle two weeks of this. I'm going home tomorrow.* After the world's fastest shower, I turn off the water and wrap myself in my beach towel. The air is so hot and humid and still inside the cabin that I decide to not dry off all the way and to sleep naked. I drape the towel over my backpack and pull my own sheet and pillow from my board bag. I spread them out on the bed. Then, naked and damp, I reach my right hand under the lampshade to turn out the light.

Before my fingers find the switch, my hand gets sucked toward the lamp and clamps around the base. I am naked with bare feet, standing in a small puddle of water on a tile floor. Electric current races through my hand, up my arm, and out to the rest of my body. It is *incredibly* painful. *I'm going to die,* I think. *I'm going to die right here, electrocuted.*

I know I am seconds from passing out. Time slows down. *I'm going to pass out and crack my head open on this tile,* I think. I angle my body so my back faces the bed. I'm going down soon, and I want to land on the bed. I use my left hand to grab the lamp and rip it from my right hand; I throw it across the room. And I pass out.

I wake up in the dark to an insect crawling across my face. It has prickly legs. I brush it off me; it feels like a huge cockroach, hard and scaly. I begin to cry for the second time since I arrived. I am lying on my back, diagonally across the bed, my feet hovering inches from the floor, my thighs and lower legs dangling off the bed, the only parts of my body on the mattress are from my butt to my shoulders, and my head hangs backward over the side near the bottom right corner. I begin to cry harder. *I'm alive,* I think. *I want to go home.* I cry some more. *You can go home first thing tomorrow,* I tell myself. *You are so tired. You must get some sleep.* I sit up and turn my body in the right direction so that my head will be on my pillow. I lie down again and will myself to sleep.

I sleep heavily and for not very long. I wake to screaming and have no idea where I am. I am wet with sweat and open my eyes to see the faint glow of sunrise coming through the cut-out hole in my hut, my window. I get up quickly and shuffle over to the window to look out . . .

The. Most. Perfect. Left point break. I have ever seen in my *life* is firing outside my window. Literally outside. Like two steps and a two-minute paddle. There are only two guys in the lineup, and they are screaming their heads off with delight. My heart begins to pound. A huge smile spreads across my face. I rip my board bag apart, grab my fins, screw them into my board, throw on a bikini and some sunblock, grab my leash, and run outside.

I ended up staying for two weeks. I made wonderful friends. Friends who left presents outside my door daily: mangoes, extra bottles of water, shells, little figurines woven from palm fronds . . . I surfed every day until I was too tired to paddle anymore. I ate delicious food and rode amazing waves. Waves so clear and so glassy that I could see every detail of the coral and every color of the fish below me *while* I was riding them.

I even found a mentor: an older man who coached me to surf on smaller boards once an Australian guest borrowed and buckled my longboard. My mentor was traveling with a quiver of close to ten boards, all marked with the logo of a well-known outdoor-gear company. In fact, all his clothing had the same logo.

Jeez, this man really loves that company, I thought.

He didn't talk much, which was fine by me. I had learned to love silences with my father, so I sat next to him at meals and was comfortable barely speaking. I liked his energy and his kind face. A shaman would say our energetic signatures were aligned. I was drawn to him and at ease in his energy field, as I could tell he was in mine.

When this man did speak, each thing he had to say was fascinating. He told me he had traveled the whole world, *way* off the beaten path. He told me about doing a trek through the mountains of India and Tibet, looking for the yeti. He told me he started a rock-climbing accessory and clothing company because he could not find—and had to make his own—gear for adventures as extreme as his. And he told me that once he realized his life would be one of travel, he decided to drink the water and eat the local foods everywhere he went.

He got really sick at first, as his body rebuilt the bacteria we are supposed to have in our gut (but that drinking our chemical-laden "treated" water in the United States kills) and then had an iron stomach. He even told me about being so poor and so hungry that when the local fishermen in Mexico caught a shark, he asked if he could keep the carcass and eat what was stuck to the bones. He found an old, empty, working refrigerator and shoved the carcass in, eating from it for days.

I was twenty-one when I heard these stories and decided then and there to do the same. I decided if I was truly going to live freely in this world, I could not be afraid of germs or illness; I had to trust my body to build up immunity. I had been so sick as a child and adolescent. I was chronically underweight, and my mother kept me filled with antibiotics. I suffered through mononucleosis multiple times, hepatitis twice, tonsillitis every year, and even got diagnosed with chronic fatigue syndrome. The moment I felt sick, my mother took me to a doctor and the doctor put me on medication.

It wasn't until I read *Diet: A Complete Guide to Nutrition and Weight Control for Dancers* by Robin D. Chmelar and Sally S. Fitt in college that I began to understand the role nutrition played in my health. And it wasn't until I read *Heal Your Body* by Louise Hay, *Way of the Peaceful Warrior* by Dan Millman, and *Anatomy of the Spirit* by Caroline Myss that I took control of my health. I changed my eating habits, changed my mental paradigm on health and wellness, and stopped going to doctors when I got sick. I endured some very rough colds and flus as my body built up the immunity to handle them on my own, but it worked. I became incredibly healthy. And when I heard these words from my new mentor, I knew I had to take my faith in my body's ability to process germs and illness and heal itself to the next level so that I, too, could travel all over the world and not get sick. It worked. I can travel anywhere and eat practically anything and not get sick. When I first heard about COVID-19, I knew to the core of my being I had nothing to fear. In fact, I traveled so much from March 2020 to October 2020 that I earned Premier 1K status on United. My goal was to get exposed as soon as possible in order to upgrade my immune system. It took spending so much of my life sick for me to find a different way. And once I did, I felt invincible.

But I didn't know these truths the year before. And I almost died—twice—in Nepal . . .

CHAPTER 14

Nepal

I knew nothing about Nepal. Seriously. This was before the internet. If I had wanted to learn about Nepal, I would have had to go to the library and look through an encyclopedia. I didn't want to do that, no interest. I just listened to the photographer when he told me I needed good hiking boots, thermal underwear, a subzero sleeping bag, a lightweight backpack, and various outer layers. I didn't train to trek for three weeks; he told me he would hire a Sherpa to carry my gear. I was, after all, the talent. My job was to strip into a bikini in all kinds of climates and look pretty. I wasn't supposed to lug shit up a mountain, or mountains.

As we made our approach to land in Kathmandu, the pilot told us we could see Mount Everest if we looked out the left side of the plane. I looked out. I didn't see anything until my boyfriend told me to look *up*. Wow! I mean, just *wow!* I mean, wow, wow, wow, wow, wow! How do you even put a mountain like that into words? The sheer size of it! The immensity! The tall, white-capped, lone jagged peak. The energy coming off it was mind-blowing. Its presence seemed to whisper, "I have been here since the beginning of eternity and will be here until the end. I am unmovable. I am majestic. I am not of this world." All I could think was, *I cannot believe people* climb *that!*

Our descent suddenly became more aggressive as we bumped and bounced our way back down to earth and landed with a skid and a lurch in Kathmandu.

Kathmandu was wild. The sheer assault on the senses was as overpowering as the view of Mount Everest. Dust filled every facial cavity I had. Cars went whizzing by on dirt roads, causing the dirt to rise in clouds so thick pedestrians could not see five feet in front of them. Yaks and cows walked among the people and the traffic, stopping to shit in *huge*, stinky, splattery piles anywhere they pleased. Families of five or six rode by crammed onto one rusty old moped. No helmets. No shoes. Vagrants lined the sidewalk, many of them missing limbs. Beggars wandered in and out of traffic, popping their deformed faces and arms into cars, pleading for food or money. So many people missing body parts, so many people deformed, so many apparent accidents that could never be mended in a hospital, left to heal without help. It broke my heart. It was almost too much to take in.

Huts lined the streets, the proprietors selling various wares. The meat huts were the worst: buckets full of animal legs, displays of animal heads, hunks of animal meat hanging, all of it dripping blood and swarming with flies and stench. The noise, the smell, the sights were so overpowering. Trash was *everywhere*. I even noticed people squatting behind huge piles of it to defecate, in the middle of the day, in wide view of all. And most apparent of all, there was so *much* color.

The buses were huge and covered with ornaments and Hindu deities, bells, and streamers. They were painted in a mix of every bright color possible, and they were *crammed* with people. People piling out the windows, people piled *on top*! People piling out the door. The clothing huts displayed brightly colored yak blankets, ponchos, and saris; the pinks, blues, yellows, greens, and oranges hanging in clumps and layers from every possible angle on every possible nail, all of it coated in dust. Skinny dark boys on bicycles dragging food carts, doughy balls of something sweet, covered in dust and flies. And in the background of all this chaos, those majestic white mountains. *Way* off in the distance. Forming a jagged wall of white. Impossibly far away, impossibly pristine, and impossibly white.

We found a guesthouse and spent the night. The photographer located a Sherpa, and the next day we were to start our three-week trek into the Himalayas. Did you notice that I said "a" Sherpa? One. The photographer decided he didn't want to pay for two. He wanted to pay for only one. So I was to put my belongings in his pack with his things, and the Sherpa would carry his pack.

One, *totally* not fair to this Sherpa.

And two, um, hello, this was not part of the plan.

But I was young. And had no boundaries. And never considered hiring my own Sherpa. Or even training to carry my own stuff. So I agreed. Which sucked, because then I was stuck. And feeling strange from the start. Something about having a stranger lug my expensive gear and supplies tugged at my heart. Something about it felt wrong. And yet I knew this was this man's livelihood.

As we got farther up into the mountains, we passed Sherpas carrying all kinds of things. Cases full of Coca-Cola strapped to their heads. Furniture—strapped to their heads! *Refrigerators!* I kid you not. Strapped to their *heads.* And when I say "strapped to their heads," I mean a thick, handmade strap that went over the head and then around and down under the *refrigerator* so that the Sherpa could carry it on his back. A fucking refrigerator. And not a mini fridge you would see in a motel. A *real* refrigerator. I mean, how?

Oh, and they were barefoot or wearing rubber flip-flops. Flip-flops! To climb the Himalayan mountains! With a refrigerator strapped to their heads! And this explains some of the deformity.

If that thing falls, when that thing falls, on a bare foot! No more foot. And it made me sad. And it made me feel even more strange. Like here we tourists were, paying money to "trek" in our expensive gear—I mean, my shoes cost more than the Sherpas would make in a lifetime—and we were paying and training for months to travel the route they walked daily to survive. And not only to survive, but to lug in all the stupid shit tourists demand. Like Coca-Cola.

In Kathmandu I was told that if we wanted warm water with which to bathe, the owners of the guesthouses would get wood and build a fire to heat the water. Which meant cutting down trees. Which meant deforestation. I vowed to go without warm water. For three weeks. In the fucking snow. Outside. And this is what I mean by "in the snow" and outside:

Our first stop was a hut. Probably twenty feet by twenty feet. It was made with two-by-fours nailed together, with *huge* gaps in between. There was a rickety rectangular wooden table with six wobbly wooden chairs, and there were five wooden platforms that served as beds. Each held an old yak blanket and nothing more.

The shower area was a much smaller hut about thirty feet away. The same size as the outhouse. Large enough for one tiny person. (The people in this area of the world were all my size: around one hundred pounds and five foot three or maybe a bit more.) The shower hut was also made of wooden planks nailed together with large gaps in between. The roof was a piece of corrugated metal placed on top. It flew off if the wind picked up. When it was snowing, the snow, along with the *freezing-cold wind*, blew between the gaps as I stood naked and shivering with a metal bucket of ice-cold water and a soup ladle. The hut had enough floor space for the bucket and me side by side and not much more. So I had to scoop a few ladles of freezing-cold water to get my body wet. Stand there wet and freezing as snow blew in. Then use the yak soap to scrub my body, more snow blowing in, and then use the ladle of cold water to rinse off the soap. I did this daily for two weeks. *Two weeks*. When done, I put on my clean thermal underwear. I had been allowed to bring one extra pair. I wore the dirty ones each day and the clean ones at night. I mean, yuck. Putting on the same dirty, dusty, sweaty, smelly socks and thermal underwear each day. Clearly I have never been homeless or a soldier.

And the walking. Every single time we would round a corner, I would pray for the terrain to level out. *Please, just be flat for a bit.* But we would turn the corner and see up, up, up. For *weeks!* Matt (my boyfriend and "chaperone") and I would wake up in the morning and joke, "What are we doing today? Oh yeah, we're walking." All day. Sunrise to sunset. Up, up, up. But I have to say: to see those white mountains looming in the distance and then to suddenly be in them, climbing them, surrounded by them, was mind-blowing. We took it one day at a time, one step at a time. And it was on this trek that I realized the photographer was just a rich guy who wanted to pay people to travel with him. Who wanted to pay pretty girls to travel with him. I don't think he had counted on my mother insisting that my boyfriend come along so that I wouldn't be in the middle of nowhere with a stranger. (This was *way* before the days of Google.) He was also a pathological liar and an alcoholic. So he would start drinking at lunch and lag behind. He would roll into our camp just as it got dark.

Except when he didn't. On the most important night. The night we made it to the last camp before "the Pass." And by "the Pass," I mean the ten-to-twelve-hour hike that went up over 22,000 feet high and then down the other side. The Pass you had to get over early, before the wind came up, or you would die. The Pass you had to get over early before a storm came, or you would die. The Pass on which he left us stranded. Because he didn't show up.

A few nights before we got to this last camp, we picked the camp below it to stop. The plan was to hike high and sleep low for two nights. To acclimatize, to get used to the altitude. We had no oxygen with us, no trekking poles. No *first aid supplies*. I mean, I had not even known where Nepal was before we landed there. So we hiked high and slept low for two days and nights, as we had been told. Everyone was fine. No altitude sickness in our group. And then we began the hike to the final stop before the Pass.

Matt and I started early, as we always did, and we got there by midafternoon. I took my usual freezing-cold "shower." The kind host got it from the river, which, by the way, was *under* a layer of ice that he graciously cracked. I returned to the camp, which consisted of one cabin with five platform beds. Again.

No one from our group showed up. *No one.* Which meant I had no gear. No sleeping bag, no food, no extra water, no tampons (I had started my period), nothing. The temperature was *way* below freezing. Our sleeping bags were cocoon bags. Meaning only enough space for one person lying on her back and also meaning for weather so severe that said person had to pull the string of the sleeping bag opening so tight the bag cinched around the head and face of the occupant, leaving only the nose or nose and mouth out to breathe. Matt and I could not share his bag. And yet, whoever was not in the bag was stuck under a pile of disgusting, smelly, filthy, dusty, *heavy* yak blankets and at risk of developing frostbite. Which meant not sleeping. Which meant staying up moving. The day before the most difficult physical trial we had ever attempted. With no training. No oxygen. And no guide. I write this now and cannot believe I got myself into this situation.

We took turns in the sleeping bag, about an hour at a time, so that we got some sleep. And when the sun began to rise, we had a decision to make: continue up and cross over the pass or backtrack and go back down the way we had come. But backtracking meant not getting much warmer. It meant not getting fed well. It meant probably running into the rest of our group and turning back around to where we now were.

For the two weeks prior we had passed people going the other way, coming from the other side of the Pass. "Warm water and apple pie," they told us. Repeatedly. The other side of the Pass was easier to get to, so there were many more supplies. They spoke of sitting to eat at tables that had warm coals by their legs. Clean sheets, and actual beds, fires and warm water, inside bathrooms and warm apple pie. We had been chanting this for ten days. "Warm water, apple pie, warm water, apple pie," as we climbed. It became our mantra. It became our dream. It became our obsession. And we could get there that night. We could get there. After that last freezing-cold, miserable, scary night, we could get there. The temptation was too much; we went for it.

And yet we didn't know. We had no idea. We didn't know our water would freeze. We didn't know the trail would be covered over with snow. We didn't know that sharing Matt's meager food supplies would not be enough to power our limbs when the oxygen level was so low. We had *zero* idea what we were in for, or how dangerous it was.

And as we climbed and climbed, the reality of the situation hit us, and the fear set in and became almost debilitating. Our water was frozen. We had nothing to drink. I was bleeding through my clothing, no matter how much toilet paper I stuffed in my panties. And then we began vomiting. At one point Matt's legs collapsed. He, after all, was carrying a full pack. We both began crying. And then we got up. "We have no option," we said. We must continue.

And continue we did. We found donkey poop and then more donkey poop and we followed it. We took three steps forward and slid two steps back, and we continued. Our faces were pink and frozen. Our tears froze before they could roll all the way down our cheeks. And we continued. One step and then another, one step and then another, one step and then another. For hour after hour after hour after hour. Surrounded by white. At the top of the world. We were 22,000 feet high. We kept going, knowing we had to. Knowing if we stopped, we would die. We got to the top before the wind came up. And we saw smoke rising. Way down below, so far away it didn't seem real, or possible to get to, we saw smoke, and we knew we had made it.

The other hikers had not been telling tall tales. There really were real beds and clean sheets, warm water, and hot apple pie. We could wash our filthy clothing in a sink! And I could wrap myself in a clean towel and crawl under clean sheets.

The photographer did not show up for three days. *Three days!* And when he did, I didn't even ask where he had been. I didn't care. I asked for my belongings. I got my tampons and my sleeping bag, and my food supplies and extra clothing. It turns out a storm had rolled in the very afternoon we had crossed the Pass, and no one could cross it for three days. But we didn't care. We had made it. And we were leaving.

The next day Matt and I left. We began walking down. I put my gear inside my sleeping bag and carried it in front of me like a baby. I trekked for days like this. Until I found a plane. Imagine that! The most rickety, rusted, dilapidated plane. Tiny. Unbearably old. And I found the pilot. And I begged for a ride out of there. We had another week to trek, and I could not do it. Not carrying my supplies like a baby in front of me. My biceps were burned out. Matt had offered to carry what he could fit in his pack, which made the weight almost intolerable to him.

We got a "yes" from the pilot. A Nepalese man. We got in this plane. It had four seats. And we took off on the tiniest runway imaginable. Which had us going full speed into the mountains. I mean, into a rock wall thousands of feet high. And at the *very last second* the pilot pulled (or pushed, I don't know how planes work) with all his might on the . . . lever that lifts the plane up . . . and the nose turned and we climbed. Skimming the mountain with our underbelly, it felt like. The most rapid acceleration I have ever experienced. Up and over the mountain and down to safety in Pokhara not much later.

Matt and I found a guesthouse and collapsed with exhaustion. And then we got sick. Violently sick. Coming out every orifice possible. Scary sick. Dehydrating sick. Utterly and totally and completely emptying-out-entirely sick. Sweating profusely. Vomiting. Diarrhea. Chills. Shaking. Trembling. Not-able-to-keep-any-water-or-food-down sick. And then weak. Not-able-to-get-out-of-bed weak. For *days*. In Pokhara. In the middle of nowhere. With no one knowing where we were.

We had made it this far to die in this bed. As we lay there soaking the mattress in the sweat we had left, a thunderstorm rolled in. And with it the lightning and thunder and then power outage. Our ceiling fan, the one saving grace, stopped rotating. The mosquitoes that had been held slightly at bay by the breeze descended on us. The heat became unbearable. And suddenly I had a vision. Of oranges. If I could get a piece of orange in my mouth, I could keep the juice down. Maybe not the actual pulp, but the juice would stay inside me. I would get some strength. I knew it. I knew my body could take it. Needed it. Craved it. Matt could not move. He was that weak.

So I got up. And I made it outside. The sun had set, and it was twilight. The town was dark because of the power outage, and it was pouring rain. The dirt streets had turned to mud, and the vendors were closing their huts and heading home. I walked as quickly as my depleted body would let me. I splashed through disgusting puddles ankle deep. And just as a vendor was closing his hut, I saw oranges. "Please," I said. "Please sell me your oranges." Which he did. All of them.

And I had been right. We could keep down the juice, which gave us strength. And when we woke up, feeling just a bit better, we could keep down the pulp. And when we felt just a bit better, we could keep down some water. And when we felt just a bit better, we ventured out for garlic soup, a local specialty. We could keep down the broth. Like this we regained our strength, and with our regained strength, we could bathe properly and wash our clothing. And in our clean clothing, with our clean bodies, we made it back to Kathmandu. And to the end of an adventure that left us forever changed.

CHAPTER 15

WOW

I believe the most difficult experiences we have to endure become our greatest teachers and cause our highest growth. I believe our soul craves adventure and *thrives* when challenged in extreme ways. And I believe there is great joy after brokenness. I say this because I know. I'm not talking about being stranded at 22,000 feet and surviving. I'm talking about finding my way back to the Light after *way* too long down in the dark.

Being shattered removes our hard edges, sands down rigid belief systems, and opens our mind to other points of view and to different ways of seeing the world, if we allow it to. When this happens, anything is possible. The magic returns, and life becomes *fun*. We discover we are so much more than we thought we were. We learn through the shattering that our rigid ways of "how the world is" need to be examined. That maybe we are not so sure how the world is, that there are still so many magical unknowns.

Kahlil Gibran says our pain is the breaking of the shell of our understanding. It's so true. We are not meant to be the same after we have been broken. We are meant to be *changed*. Expanded, different, closer to our true expression. Softer, kinder, wiser, more compassionate, and filled again with wonder. As life coach Cynthia Occelli says, "For a seed to achieve its greatest expression, it must come completely undone. The shell cracks, its insides come out, and everything changes. To someone who doesn't understand growth, it would look like complete destruction."

I think our society struggles with "kidults" because we don't go through the rites of passage indigenous peoples do. When we have been pushed to our limits and found a way to survive, we believe in ourselves. We feel safe and strong and capable. When we have not gone through these types of ordeals, we still have a need to be taken care of and protected. We don't believe we can survive on our own. It is only when we try and succeed at doing something we didn't know we could that we grow in confidence. And, as I mentioned earlier, our soul *craves* being challenged, *craves* adventure. We didn't incarnate in these human bodies to stay locked inside our homes, safe. We came for a wild ride. We didn't come here to have all the answers, to be bored because we already "know how everything works." We came here to be surprised, to not know, to experience it all, to be confused, to be amazed, to be *thrilled*.

I heard once that a spiritual master knew he was going to die and had his students gather around to watch him go into a state of deep meditation and leave his body. "Kick the frame" they used to call it. Before he closed his eyes to meditate, a student asked, "Master, how would you sum up your time on Earth?" The master thought for a moment, smiled, eyes twinkling with memories, with love and light, and then said one word: "Wow!"

PART 3

SPIRIT

Some people will never like you
because your spirit irritates their demons.

—DENZEL WASHINGTON

CHAPTER 16

MaNta Ray

It's midmorning in Hawaii, on a beautiful summer day. The ocean appears calm, deep dark blue, with light dancing and sparkling on the surface. The air is warm and a slight breeze lifts the shorter pieces of hair that fall around my face as I crawl into Noah's boat. Holding on to the splintered wooden piling, I lower one leg, get my footing on the deck, and shift my weight to get the rest of me in; a yellow mesh bag of snorkel gear dangles from my right hand. I am wearing a tiny blue bikini with a pink flowered sarong tied around my waist, little black rubber Locals flip-flops on my feet.

As soon as I'm in the boat, I dump my gear and help Noah untie the lines, leaving them behind on the dock, tied around the pilings, for easy tie-up when we return. He smiles at me as I settle in next to him behind the steering console, and away we go, heading out of Hale'iwa Harbor and making our way around Kaena Point.

The ocean is smooth, so Noah keeps the boat at close to full throttle. The wind whips and tangles my hair, the saltwater splashes me from the bow, cooling me off and coating my sunglasses with film. We don't try to talk over the buzz of the engine; instead, we sit side by side in companionable silence, the way boat people do.

My mind drifts to random thoughts: *It's so beautiful. I love my life. This reminds me of childhood. I wonder if we'll be back in time for ballet class . . .* I allow the thoughts to flow through, not giving any of them much attention, as Noah slows the boat a bit. We had entered much deeper water, and the swells coming around the point are making the high speed dangerous. They roll beneath us, making us climb slightly up and then slightly back down the cobalt-blue waves.

I know this type of water from countless ocean crossings when I was a kid, and I step to the side of the boat, hold on to a stanchion, and peer into the water, hoping to see flying fish or a dolphin. I scan below us, then behind us, and finally turn my gaze ahead. Immediately, I spot a manta ray off our starboard bow. She is *huge*. And magnificent. Weighing roughly three thousand pounds, with a wingspan of something close to twenty feet, larger than the boat. My heart races. It is rare to see a manta so close to the surface. I want to be with her, to see her better.

Impetuously, and without saying a word to Noah, I grab my mesh bag from the deck, pull out my mask, and jump off the side of the moving boat, into the water. I simply *have* to be closer to this glorious creature. Immediately the current catches me. The thought *My father told me to always wear dive fins when I'm in the water; never jump in without fins* explodes into my head. And this is why. I am in very deep water, with no dive fins and no ability to swim against the current. I am helpless.

The manta senses my presence. I have landed maybe fifteen feet from her right wing, and she slowly and gracefully turns her huge body to look at me. In a flash, she and I are face-to-face. Her mouth, easily four feet wide, is open, and I realize only then that she could swallow me whole if she wants to. She could crush me with one swipe of her massive wing. She could pull me down and drown me. I have a moment of intense fear, and then I relax into safety. I feel so safe. My heart leaps with adrenaline and awe at being so close to such a massive and magnificent creature, and my soul is *overwhelmed* with love for her.

Everything around me goes quiet. Time stands still. I love her *so* much. With all of me. I don't know why. I just do. And she seems to know it. I realize now animals are wide-open portals to the divine. They are vortexes of Pure Love. And this manta was a *humungous* portal. I had landed in her vortex and was immediately enveloped in her vibration.

She stays with me, facing me, as the current sweeps us both rapidly out to sea. I am in awe of her, and she seems to be fascinated by me. I could stay here, with her, forever. I notice the sheer size of her. The thickness of her skin. I notice the stark contrast between the bright white of her belly and the dark black of her back and wings. I can see inside her wide-open mouth. I see the outline of the bones of her ribs. And she angles herself a bit so that she can see me with one of those massive eyeballs. My mind keeps chanting, *I love you so much, I love you so much, I love you so much,* and I feel the current of love flowing out of me toward her. My heart seems ready to explode with love, so much is flowing through me. We float like this, facing each other, barely moving, taking each other in.

But an engine noise breaks the spell. Noah has turned the boat around and is coming back to get me. The roar and buzz are getting louder, and I know she will flee momentarily. I say goodbye to her in my mind, and as if on cue, she dives deep. The dark black of her body disappears quickly into the deep blue of the sea. She is so *fast.* I stay looking down, watching her go, as Noah maneuvers the boat close enough to grab me, yelling at me as he does. I look up. He's pissed.

I reach my arm up, and he yanks me into the boat. "You're fucking crazy," he screams. "Don't ever do that again!"

"She was amazing," I say, removing my mask and snorkel to do so.

"I don't care," he spits back. "What you did was absurd! So dangerous! Never, *ever* jump off a boat without telling the captain!"

"I'm sorry," I say. And I mean it, understanding how reckless and irresponsible my actions had been. "I won't do it again."

He shakes his head. "You are seriously fucking nuts." He laughs.

No argument there. No impulse control, either. But, somehow, my heart had told my body I would be safe. And so I was.

CHAPTER 17

Seeker

All throughout history there have been wars. There have always been people hating those who are different. And there have always been far too many who have used their positions of power and influence to manipulate, oppress, and kill those with less power. I will never understand it. However, I do know that we all incarnate over and over. And that we must experience and endure everything to which we have subjected another. So, I cannot help but wonder why people want to be so cruel to each other when we are here for such a short time. And when they will have to have inflicted upon them *all* that they have done to others. For some this is signing up for thousands and thousands of lifetimes of hardship and ill treatment. For a rare few, millions.

I think of the witch trials of the past. And I wonder what it is that makes humans want to demonize and kill that which they do not understand. And not only kill, but torture. Look at what happened to Jesus. Look at what happens to almost all prophets. I wonder why those of us who speak of magic and miracles seem to be the most threatening. Like maybe if the masses knew life was magic and all part of a divine plan, they could not be so easily controlled by messages of fear, and those who seek to control want to prevent this sovereignty at all costs.

This world is not what we are taught in school and in most religions. It is so much more. I had to go find that out for myself. I traveled all the time, slept with so many men, and joined a Buddhist cult because I was lost and searching. My spirit was dying. The lack-based, scarcity-based, fear-based paradigms I had been taught made my soul ache. And the accepted paradigms of the world made no sense to me. They never resonated as truth.

I used to think "seeker" meant "lost soul." Someone wandering around sad, forlorn, not fitting into human life on Earth. But what I eventually came to know is "seeker" means someone who remembers. Someone who remembers a promise of magic and miracles, a promise of always being connected to Source Energy, a promise of never being alone, never being without guidance, never being without love.

I knew from a very young age that what I was learning in church did not make sense. If God created us, how could we be created as sinners? That made zero sense to me. If God created the universe and everything in it, how could God make such a mistake with each one of us? The adults had holes in their logic. To me it only made sense that God would create each one of us *perfectly.*

And that God would love us and want us to be happy. As a child I imagined God was the one who made me love cheese, and my family, and ballet dancing. I knew it was God who planted my desires into my heart, so how could following my desires be wrong? Following them had to be right. The idea that our Creator would smite us and damn us for following our desires made no sense to me. The idea that we were "born sinners" seemed to me, in my five-year-old brain, like the adults were saying God made really bad drawings with ugly colors and lots of mistakes. I figured then the adults had to be wrong. If I had to pick who was right, I would pick God. At five years old I knew a secret the adults didn't know: *we aren't sinners.*

Now that I knew the adults were wrong about something as huge as this, I began to question everything. As I got a bit older, marriage didn't make sense to me. The idea of it scared me. I liked a lot of boys. How could I pick one *for life*? And how would I know which one to pick? And if I couldn't be intimate with him until *after* I picked him . . . well, how would I know if we fit? This seemed backward to me.

And I looked at the married adults I knew, and they seemed bored. A lot of them seemed to hate each other. They sure didn't talk very nicely to each other. They sure didn't get the red face and glow when they saw each other, the way I did when I saw George Zinkler or Gordon Breslav. And if I did end up with George Zinkler or Gordon Breslav for life, I would want him to be free to leave me any time he wanted to. I would never want someone I loved stuck to me just because he signed a contract.

I thought about this a lot. Why, in a world of billions of people, would we tie ourselves to just one, *for life*? And how could we possibly know who would fit for life, when we don't even know ourselves? At this young age I simply knew I would *never* be able to make that decision. The idea of not being able to be free to explore the world and discover who I was, that I would be tied to someone and have to make all my decisions with that person in mind, that I couldn't trade that person in if we no longer fit well, or if he got mean, terrified me. Plus, I knew if I tried it, I would fail. I loved cupcakes, but if someone told me I had to eat them three times a day, every day, until death, I would *hate* them. They would go from bringing me joy to making me sick. I knew I would never be able to promise I would stay with someone until death. So when the other little girls played "wedding" and "marriage," I imagined sailing around the world in a sailboat.

When my hormones really kicked in and my Catholic mother told me women only have sex to please men, I knew I had to go out and have as much sex as possible. Just to find a different truth. The church had told me sex was dirty and evil. My mother said it was no fun. And yet it sure felt good when *I* touched those parts of my body. The energy stirring in me when I saw a boy I had a crush on definitely did not feel dirty or evil. It felt *thrilling*. It felt *fun*. It made me feel alive in a way I had never before experienced. And it felt like *love*.

How could the part of my body that creates new life be shameful or dirty? How could uniting this part with someone I loved be wrong? Why would our Creator make this union of two bodies feel so pleasurable if we were not meant to do it? This made no sense to me. Plus, my mother seemed *miserable*. The people in church seemed *miserable*. And the dried-up old white guy preaching this stuff seemed like he had not smiled in decades. Like he had zero life in him. Like he needed to get *laid*.

On and on it went. With each mainstream, mass-consciousness paradigm I learned, I felt a *deep* sadness in my bones. An ache. A soul ache. It seemed everyone outside of me was saying, "This is the way it is. This is the way it is. This is the way it is . . ." And everything inside of me was *screaming*, "No, it's not; no, it's not; no, it's not!"

CHAPTER 18

Hawaiian Waterfall

I'm camping in Hawaii with two girlfriends. We have no idea what we are doing or where we are going, but we sure are having a lot of fun. Drinking wine, running around naked in the moonlight, laughing until our cheeks hurt. We wake up at sunrise and decide to follow a donkey trail to a waterfall. We get lost and end up deep in the tropical jungle. My friends want to turn back, but I want to keep going. I can hear the waterfall, and it sounds massive.

Just as we are deciding what to do, a man comes out of the dense foliage. He is small and brown. Wiry. Old. He has thinning short gray hair and is wearing a tattered T-shirt and worn, faded shorts. He is barefoot and holds a massive machete in his right hand. And even though he is small, he exudes power and prowess. He is animal-like, as if he could jump twenty feet straight up and cling to a palm tree. In fact, he may have just been doing that, using the machete to cut down coconuts.

His sudden appearance scares my friends, and their fear startles him. He scowls and quickly scurries around them. "Excuse me,"

I say as he passes. "We are looking for the waterfall. Is this the correct trail to get there?" I ask him. And I smile. I remove my sunglasses and look into his eyes, cloudy with age and lifelong exposure to blinding sunlight. He stops, and his contracted energy expands. I feel it and see it. This being is massive. And magical. His face lights up with a nearly toothless smile, and he says to me, "You scared me." Which surprises me. But then I realize that white people are scary to indigenous peoples, with good reason, and that thought makes my heart sad for a moment, makes me ashamed of my skin color. "You scared us," my friends say back. He smiles at them. That charming lightbulb of a smile. And he says, "Me? A harmless old man?" His look and his voice are mischievous. We all giggle, standing almost smashed together in the dense jungle, with large vibrant green elephant ear leaves protruding from the plant hanging over his head. "Come," he says. "I will take you." My heart leaps. I cannot wait to go on an adventure with this man. I smile at my friends.

As we follow him, I notice mangoes on a tree and stop to get one. I run to catch up with them and eat it as we walk, peeling the skin off with my teeth and spitting it into the jungle. A little later I notice guava on a tree and grab one. I crack it open and eat the inside, throwing the shell into the trees. I'm the last in our line of four. Stopping and catching up, stopping and catching up. Our fearless leader has not broken stride. I notice mountain apples and grab a few, eating them as we go. Saying "thank you" in my mind each time a tree yields her fruit to me. Asking permission in my mind each time before I take. The Carlos Castañeda books taught me to always ask a plant permission before I touch her or take from her. I have never been told no.

Next we pass papayas. One looks ready to fall but is too high for me to reach. "Excuse me," I say. "Any way you could help me get that papaya? It looks perfect." He begins to laugh. "I will get it for you, Hungry." He continues with, "I am naming you Hungry. For someone so little, you sure do eat a lot." I turn red and smile. "I can't resist when they look so ripe," I say. He leaps into the air and hits the orange papaya with his machete. He catches it as it falls and hands it to me. "Thank you," I say, and put it in my backpack to share with the others when we have our lunch.

Twenty minutes later we reach the fall, which is enormous, and roaring, and mind-numbingly loud, and we sit down on large black lava rocks that circle a pond of blue-green water. The spray from the fall coats us. Our guide goes off walking while we pull out sandwiches from our bags. When he returns, I offer him half of mine. He smiles and extends his hand, takes a bite, makes a happy face, and then asks us if we would like to swim. "Yes!" we respond.

He hands me a Ti leaf he has just plucked and says we must ask the water if we may enter her. He tells me to ask the water if we may swim and then to place the Ti leaf gently on the surface. "If it sinks, you may not swim. If it stays afloat, you have been given permission," he explains. I ask the water and gently place the Ti leaf on her surface. It stays afloat, and we all smile. We finish our sandwiches, peel off our sweaty socks, shorts, and shirts, and enter the cold water in our bikinis.

Once we submerge, he says to us, "Would you like to go behind the waterfall?" I look at the fall; it is colossal. I'm not sure exactly what he means, or how we would even get past it. To me it looks like it comes crashing down the face of the rock wall. How would we get behind it? "I think so," I say to him. "But how?"

He tells us to wait for him, to wait for his signal, that we will know it when we see it, and once we do, to swim toward the fall. This man is quite mysterious. He swims out toward the crashing water and disappears underneath. We watch. Where did he go? Is he okay? We wait. And then we notice the intensity of the waterfall begins to subside. Where there was crashing, raging water, swirling foam, and a high dense mist, there is now only a curtain of water gentle enough to show our guide standing behind it.

This is obviously the signal, so we swim toward him, dive down underneath, and come up behind the fall, where there is a cave. It's amazing back here. The man smiles his toothless grin, wide and full. His face lights up. "I had a feeling she would allow you here," he says to us. I don't ask how he did what he did. None of us does. Somehow we know not to ask. It would ruin the moment.

We explore the cave, allow the water to fall on our heads like a shower. Then we begin to get cold and tell him we are going to swim back to the rocks on the far side, where we had entered the pool. Which we do. As we get out, we turn around, shivering in the sun. The waterfall gets louder and louder, stronger and stronger, crashing once again. And our guide appears on our side of it. He comes to join us on our rocks in the sun and helps us open the papaya with his knife. We smile and eat in silence. Then Carrie asks, "How did you do that?" He doesn't respond. He chews his piece of the papaya. He turns to look at the waterfall. And then he says, "I just asked."

CHAPTER 19

JONAH

I never did have the ménage à trois with the twenty-four-year-olds. I was never the meat in that tennis player sandwich. I mean, where would all the penises go? Certainly not in my body. It seemed like a lot of work. Like I was the one who would be doing all the work. Like I would be servicing *them*. I remember sex with twenty-four-year-olds. The jackhammer into the bed. The straddling my face, never waiting for me to initiate that kind of intimacy. I remember it all being over in five minutes. No thanks. Not for me. Not anymore.

Something registered on my radar. Something said, "He's kind and he's nice and he has a sweet heart and he's interesting and financially secure and famous, but I'm being used. I would be used." My days of being used are over.

But it didn't save me. I still spiraled into a hell of self-doubt and regret. I spent a *week* in darkness. Should I have slept with him? Is he my soul mate? Should I go back to Florida? I mean, come *on*.

Seriously? After all I have lived through, after all I had become, this is what I was thinking? This is the state I was in?

In my confusion and sadness, I became convinced the only way I could be happy was with him. Going back to Sarasota to be with him. I became convinced my life as an author had hit a wall and the book was going nowhere. Somehow I got so out of alignment that I didn't want to live in Colorado and I didn't want to write and I just wanted to go surfing and date a twenty-four-year-old. Move to Sarasota. I mean, what the *hell*? How does someone my age who has gone through all I've gone through get that lost? It faded. Thankfully. And I got my clarity back. And I was able to see Jonah as just this beautiful magical gift that entered my life at the exact right time to help me get over a breakup and also to show me what it's like to be with someone who is thriving and loves his life. And that was it. I'm sure I helped him with stuff he was struggling with, too. We were gifts in each other's lives, and then we were *meant* to go our separate ways. The guy I had just broken up with said to me, as we were breaking up, "When the flow of the universe pulls us apart, we have to honor it. To disregard it and try to hang on is what sours a relationship." I loved him for his wisdom and the grace with which he let go, especially since I was the one ending it.

Leaving that boyfriend was not easy. It's hard to let go of something that is wonderful just because you get a sense deep in your gut that it doesn't feel right. The mind makes all kinds of lists. Friends talk you into staying. And yet my heart will not let me betray myself any longer. The signals with him got louder and louder until my hand ached when he held it and I cringed when he walked into my house. Not because he wasn't amazing. He was. Simply because on some level our souls made the choice to move in different directions. And so we honored it. We *had* to.

With the hot young tennis players, I said no, because I knew where that path led. I said no because I didn't want to be used to check off boxes on some boys' lists. I said no because I finally have my own back, because I finally have boundaries, because I finally know who I am and what I want. In the blur of drunkenness, in the height of all that tequila hitting me, in the spinning and the swaying and the nebulous focus, I stopped time and checked in with myself: *Do I want to do this or do I not?* The answer was a very clear no.

Then I asked myself, *With just Jonah, do I want to do this or do I not?* And again the answer was still no. Not as clear, some temptation there, the need to be held, the desire to follow the electricity, the instinct to want the passion. But I sensed how it would play out. I sensed someone using me to check a box. Older woman. Check. Woman who doesn't live here and will not bother me. Check. I got a visual of the play-out. Not intimate. Not loving. Not bonding. Just sex. The kind where the man doesn't really touch you with his body. No trying to get as close as two bodies will allow. No blending two humans into one. No lining up chakras and combining energy and Light to create something so much more magnificent than the sum of the parts. Just penis in vagina or other orifices. I didn't want that. I don't want that. My time doing that is done. I can't say done forever. I don't know. But I do know that right now I crave connection. I crave bonding. I crave love.

Those boys asked me, "Aren't you looking for great sex?" and my answer, in all my drunkenness, was "I'm looking for love." I didn't say, "No, I'm not looking for great sex." I mean, who out there is *not* looking for great sex? I just knew I needed love first. *Know* I need love first. No more betraying myself. No more pretending. No more going after a half-assed version of something that looks like it could maybe be something I want. Like sex with a stranger, hoping it could turn into love.

I had regrets after. The next day. The next few days. *Maybe I should have,* I thought. *Maybe I was wrong. Maybe it would have been great. Maybe sex with a young guy is exactly what I need.* But I know myself now. And I know I would have been sad. That I would have been kind of into it until I had an orgasm, and then I would have felt very sad. I would have wanted to fall asleep on his chest, loving him, bonding with him.

We women secrete a bonding hormone called oxytocin when we are physically intimate with someone. The same hormone we secrete when we breastfeed an infant. It's biological. To bond us to our children. And yet so many of us pretend we can have meaningless sex and not get attached. But I'm not sure how true that is. I think we are biologically *wired* to bond with the men we allow into our bodies. We hold them. We allow them inside. And then we wrap our arms and legs around them in an embrace. To think we can do this with another human, when the deepest, truest desire of all of us is to love and be loved and *not* bond with the person, *not* want more is, in my opinion, self-betrayal on the deepest level. I can hear some of you saying, "I can totally have sex and not get attached," and I believe you. And I say, "Good for you! Great for you. I wish I were that woman, but I am not."

Men are biologically wired to spread their seed as far and wide as possible. They also thrust into us and can have *only* their genitalia touch us, if that is what they want. It really can be that detached for them. I believe men can maybe have meaningless sex, but I'm really not so sure women can. But what other women can or cannot do is none of my business. What *this* woman can or cannot do is my business. And I finally know I can't just be a checkbox on someone else's list. I can't just be runner-up. I can't be fun for one night and not called again. Not anymore. And so I said no. And it still didn't save me. I had experienced enough closeness to begin a fantasy. To fall in love. To bond. We had kissed and we had embraced and we had held each other's hands. We had talked, and we had danced, and we had laughed. We had spent the day together at the beach. I left the next day, and I still did what I always do: I turned him into my soul mate inside my mind. *Maybe we could be a couple,* I thought. *Maybe the age difference doesn't matter. Maybe we* are *soul mates.*

Thank God I know myself now. So I erased his number from my phone. To save myself. Because I knew I would fall into this old pattern. Even if I didn't sleep with him. I knew, because I *didn't* know him well, that I could make him perfect in my mind. Not enough time with him to notice all the ways we don't fit. Only enough time to notice the ways we do. Which is one of my gifts. I love seeing the God inside people. I love seeing the best in them and bringing it to the surface. But it has its flaws. It makes me fall in love with everyone, and it makes me create soul mate matches in my mind, matches with people who really don't care that much about me. Sad face emoji here. But also *not* sad face. Because now I have my own back. I check in with myself. Now I know it is not up to someone else to make me happy. It is up to me. I am in charge of my happiness, of my joy, of my serenity and safety. Of my optimism and my enthusiasm for life. And I am wise now. I have hard-earned wisdom. In my twenties I would have slept with Jonah. I probably would have slept with both of them. So that they would like me. Hoping that they would love me. Hoping to hitch my wagon to theirs and be "pro-tennis-player girlfriend." Now I realize it is up to me to create a life I love. To be me regardless of whom I'm dating. To have my own boundaries. To constantly check in with myself and ask, "Do I really want this? Is this okay?"

CHAPTER 20

Mail-Order Bride

When I was twenty-one, just about to turn twenty-two, I wandered into a room full of men and accidentally became a mail-order bride. Sent to Fiji.

It was a hot, humid, sultry afternoon. I had just finished class at University of Hawaii, Manoa, and rode my bike to a friend's house, propping it up against the crumbling front stairs.

Walking unannounced through the rusty screen door, I entered the brown, Barcalounger-filled living room just as a guy I had never seen before mentions Tavarua Island in Fiji.

"I was there last summer," I piped in as the screen door slammed behind me, sending the sleeping black cat scrambling off a nearby Barcalounger. "Well, not there. Not on Tavarua. It's so expensive. But I was in Fiji for a modeling job, and we went by Tavarua a few times on the boat. The waves were firing," I say as I sit down in the spot the cat had just vacated.

We all keep talking, and it turns out this guy's friend Rick owns this island. Okay, not *owns*. A non-Fijian cannot own an island in

Fiji. But he (along with a friend of his) was granted a ninety-nine-year lease on the island by the tribe that owns it.

The new guy then tells me Tavarua is scheduled to have the first-ever tube-riding contest with some of the best surfers in the world, and they need a bikini model. Would I be interested in being that model? Um, hello, of *course* I would be interested! He agrees to pass my phone number off to Rick.

My phone number is the number to an astoundingly heavy, beige rotary dial telephone on the tiny desk of the room I had rented nearby. Well, pantry, really. I had rented a pantry. I had found a room to rent for cheap. The advertisement handwritten on an index card thumbtacked to the bulletin board outside Foodland. $150 a month. In a women's dorm. Off campus. The room I had found was, indeed, a converted pantry. It was across the hall from the kitchen, which meant I got all the noise and all the cockroaches. It was next to the door that led to our back entrance, which meant everyone who came in that way looked in my tiny window. And it was so small it held an old musty army cot (my bed), a tiny worn wooden desk and wobbly chair, and the world's smallest dresser, with a toaster on top, so I could make some food in my room and get more cockroaches.

My longboard fit inside with me, but barely. The back end with the fin went in the upper-right corner of the room, wedged against the ceiling over my cot, and the nose of the board went diagonally down and to the left, to the floor right behind my door. I had to duck under it to get into "bed" and to sit at my tiny desk. But I was twenty-one years old and living on my own in Hawaii, plus getting summer credits for college in my hope to make up for the semester I had missed traveling the world modeling. So I was happy. I was dating a ridiculously handsome Maori lifeguard I had met on the beach in Waikiki, and he was teaching me how to tandem surf with him, holding me perfectly posed high over his head once we were up and riding on a wave. I loved my pantry life in Hawaii.

In order for me to talk to Rick, I had to actually *be* in my pantry when he called. I didn't have an answering machine. Or a cell phone. Which meant a week went by with no call, followed by another week. I began to give up on going to Tavarua. However, one evening when I was toasting a veggie burger on top of the world's smallest dresser, the phone rang, and it was Rick. Over a crackling, static-filled, heavily delayed connection, I told him I would love to model, as long as there were no other expectations. "Often these types of offers come with strings attached," I said, remembering some of the horrible bikini model casting calls I had shown up to in Miami, clad in a sundress, surf bikini, and sandals only to feel humiliated when the other women appeared wearing nothing but heavy makeup, G-strings, and stilettos. He promised me his reputation was too important to be manipulating women to come to his island, told me the dates and details, and sent me a plane ticket. I was headed back to Fiji as soon as my semester ended!

At the airport in Honolulu, my traveling companions were obvious. Surf star after surf star began to show up. I had to clamp my jaw shut to keep from drooling. A few famous surf photographers arrived, along with a famous surf commentator. I shyly approached the group. "I'm Renee," I said. "I'm the bikini model." I got a few ego-boosting lingering stares.

Sam George, a famous surf journalist and the man who seemed to be in charge, glanced at a list he was holding. "Oh, you're Rick's girlfriend," he said to me.

"Um, no . . ." I responded. He gave me a strange look. And he laughed. And he turned red. He looked back down at his list. More people arrived, and he quickly got surrounded. I backed away and waited until it was time to board the plane.

Because my seat had been added so much later, I did not sit near the group on the plane but was reunited with them after we all cleared customs. A driver was waiting to take us to a café for breakfast, while we awaited a boat to take us to Tavarua. It was during breakfast that Sam approached me. He was kind and smiling, his good-humored face sun-kissed and framed by shaggy blond hair. He showed me his list: There I was at the very top. "Renee Linnell, Rick's girlfriend."

By then Sam's wife had joined us. She was as kind as Sam, and I loved her immediately. I explained to them who I really was and why I was there. I told them about the conversation I had with Rick and about meeting his friend in Manoa. We all laughed and wondered . . . was I being set up with Rick? By the time breakfast was over, they were sure I was and graciously gave me the label mail-order bride.

Mail-order bride or not, the trip was incredible. The island was only twenty-nine acres. It was lush jungle in the middle, surrounded by pristine, baby-powder-soft white sand and protected by a barrier of coral reef. From the air, the island looked like a heart.

Rick was a total gentleman. He never asked me to do anything besides model on the beach and in the water. Everyone visiting the island was fun, interesting, and kind. Not only did I get to watch the best surfers in the world ride some of the best waves in the world, but I fell in love with the Fijians, one of the friendliest peoples I had ever met.

Most of them had *huge* smiles that lit up their faces, and when they sang it melted my heart. I learned the words to their songs as quickly as possible so I could sing with them. The women wore dresses, and the men wore sarongs (long skirts) with shirts. I never saw one Fijian man in pants. The material for both genders' clothing was colorful and patterned with flowers, shells, and sea animals. The women often wore one huge red, pink, or yellow hibiscus flower tucked behind an ear, creating a beautiful contrast with their dark skin.

Because all the surfers, photographers, and commentators took up the beach bungalows, I was set up in a tree house on the far side of the island. This was Rick's personal guesthouse, and it was the most charming place I have ever stayed. To get into it, I had to climb a wooden ladder, which deposited me on a wooden walkway built on the limbs of two connecting trees. The walkway had small railings to hold me in, and the wood was sturdy enough not to flex under my feet. Ten feet from the ladder, I entered a small room with a full-size bed, a wooden dresser topped with glass, and a louver window on all four walls. The windows had little white lace curtains on either side, and the bed was covered in a white lace duvet with heart-shaped throw pillows. The room had a door on both ends and was only wide enough to fit the full-size bed next to the door on one side, the tiny dresser next to the door on the other, and long enough that I could stand between the dresser and the foot of the bed.

The door on the far side of the room led to another walkway, which led to another tiny tree house built in another tree. This one sat directly over the ocean. And it was more of a hut or a viewing area. It had a platform bed with a bare queen mattress, but only a floor and roof, so anyone sleeping there would be exposed to the elements. It had its own ladder going down to the beach.

All in all, the island had fewer than a dozen beach bungalows, two bathrooms (one for men, one for women, both with two stalls each), a restaurant, a boutique, a house for each owner (there were two of them—Jon and Rick,) a guesthouse for each owner, and "Fiji camp." To find my tree house, I had to walk through the jungle down sandy dirt paths and memorize the plants so I knew where to turn. In the beginning I made mistakes and ended up in Fiji camp or at Jon's house. To go to the bathroom, I had to walk back to the restaurant or go outside. The problem with going outside, especially at night or in the early morning, was the sea snakes. Long white-and-black-striped creatures that kill when they bite. "Don't worry about them," Rick told me. "They have tiny mouths. The only way they could kill you is if they bite a nipple or in between your fingers or toes." He knew this, the whole nipple thing, because a man had died that way. His drunk friends put a sea snake down his shirt, and it clamped onto his nipple. I decided to keep my nipples away from the snakes, but I had a decision to make: If I waded into the water to go to the bathroom, would they go for in between my toes?

I decided the answer was no, and in the early morning, when I couldn't make it all the way to the other side of the island in time, I would wade into the water under my tree house to poop. The sea snakes would swim around me, but they kept their distance. Maybe they don't love human poop. I mean, who does, really? I guess I didn't mind the snakes so much when I could see them, but nighttime was a whole different story. At night they would crawl up on land and nestle in areas that held warmth. So, for middle-of-the-night pees, I would hang my booty over the side of the walkway and pee from the air. I tried to aim in under my shower bag. A solar bag we all had that we hung from a tree. There were no showers on Tavarua, so we each got a bag. We filled it with fresh water each morning and let it sit in the sun all day—warm water to wash the salt off at night and also to wash away the pee.

It was in Fiji that I learned I could not trust the news. One day when a small group of us was in the capital city shopping, there was a coup. The government got overthrown by rebel forces. And this is how the Fijian rebels overthrew the government: they walked in, announced that they were taking over, gave the existing government time to leave, offered fruit and kava, and then took over. We noticed no disturbance in the streets. In fact, I only found out about it because I called my mother that evening from the satellite phone in the office.

"Renee, are you okay?" She was so alarmed.

"Yes, of course I am . . ."

"I see bloody bodies, guns, and rioting in the streets," she said to me.

"What are you watching?" I asked.

"The *news!*" she cried back. "There is a coup in Fiji. You have to leave. Immediately!"

"Mom," I responded. "I was there today. There is no violence. There are no guns. There are no bloody bodies." I continued. "Tell me what the people are wearing."

"What?" she asked.

"The bloody people and the people with guns, what are they wearing?" I asked.

"Torn shirts and pants," she said.

"Mom, that's not Fiji," I said back.

"What are you talking about?" she replied.

"Whatever you are watching, whatever you are seeing, that is *not* Fiji," I said.

"But the newscasters are saying, 'A coup in Fiji . . .'"

"Well, yes, Mom, there is a coup in Fiji. But there are no bloody bodies or guns, and Fijians do not wear torn T-shirts and pants."

The government got restored. There was another food and kava ceremony between the rebels and the overthrown/reinstated government, and all was well. But on that day I discovered another very important truth: I had to go out and get my own facts about the world. No more trusting the TV to tell me anything.

CHAPTER 21

INTENSE

I was telling a friend a story about the time I flew to San Jose, Costa Rica; took a bus overflowing with people, luggage, and chickens for five hours on a rickety, pothole-filled, narrow, winding, steep jungle-lined road (with thousand-foot drop-offs if a car pass went awry) to Dominical; stayed a few hours; hitchhiked *another* five hours on the same treacherous, pothole-filled (but not as steep) winding dirt road to Pavones; spent the night; got dropped off by a boat in some crazy surf; surfed until I couldn't paddle; hitchhiked all the way back to San Jose; and flew out the following day because I had sunstroke and wanted to be home in air-conditioning. I was in Costa Rica a little more than forty-eight hours and in that time traveled all the way to the Panamanian border and back, plus took a boat to Matapalo. It was a wild story. And great surf. And *terrible* sunstroke. And super-uncomfortable traveling.

And my friend looked at me with her mouth open and said, "Renee, *this* is why you freak out and need to spend so much time alone. Because you do shit like *that!*" She continued. "Who does that?" We both laughed. And then she added, "If you were a little less extreme, you would be able to manage your time out in the world and not get depleted to the point that you need to hole up as a hermit for two weeks before you can socialize again."

She was right, of course.

And yet . . .

I don't want to live any less intensely. I saw most of my family die before I turned fifteen. And my father died on Thanksgiving Day when I *was* fifteen. How do I know when my time is up? Why would I want to do anything mediocre?

That day the boat dropped me off in the surf, it was taking us all to a place called Rubber Duckies. I had never surfed there before, but as we passed a double-overhead right point break that peeled for long enough before it hit some huge rocks, I asked the captain to slow down, grabbed my board, and jumped over the side of the boat, yelling, "Pick me up on your way back."

No way was I going to surf Rubber Duckies with that empty wave right there. Fortunately for me, another passenger in the boat decided to join me. We surfed for *hours*. Until we could barely move. And then we paddled to shore, looking for shade, food, and water.

As we hit the soft white sand, two adorable blond twins appeared from the tree line. They could not have been older than six. And they invited us to their house, clearly handmade by their parents, and nestled in the shade of the jungle. The parents fed us mangoes and bananas and gave us water. We played with the children. And by the time the boat came back, I was lobster-red and dizzy, with a splitting headache. By the time I got back to my cabin, I had chills and a fever. As mosquitoes feasted on my flesh and I tossed and turned in pools of my own sweat, I fantasized about being home in my mother's house in Florida, sleeping in air-conditioning. I had spent the previous three weeks living in a tent in Mexico and had been fantasizing about beds and air-conditioning for close to a month. So when I heard an engine start up before dawn, I ran outside to see who was going where and realized I had found a ride back to the San Jose airport. A straight shot. In a nice rental car. With air-conditioning. And shock absorbers. And good tires. No bus. No more melting. No more mosquitoes. No chickens. No motion-sick passengers vomiting. My own seat. Nice car to the airport, short flight, home sweet home.

So, yes, I went to Costa Rica and traveled all the way to the Panamanian border, surfed my ass off, and went home, all in close to forty-eight hours. And yes, I'm intense. And yes, sometimes that scares people, especially men. But, as I said in the beginning of this book, I'm done pretending to be something I'm not. I'm done holding in my wings and my fire. I want to roar. I have to roar. We all do. And we have to be willing to face some destruction . . . as we melt away all that makes us small.

CHAPTER 22

ME BEING ME

When I suggest to people that they can create lives they love, most of them get angry. Why is this? Why do people argue *so strongly* for their limitations? In a world where anything is possible, in a world where people like Helen Keller can figure out a way to not only survive, but thrive, why use so much energy explaining away possibility?

A big part of me has always worried that me just being me is hurting people, is offending them, is upsetting them, is making them feel bad about themselves. And so I have attracted into my life people who *do* get offended and upset by me just being me, especially by me thriving. Friends who have always wanted to write off my optimism or any of my achievements as "she has money so it's easy for her." Disregarding the fact that I have money because I inherited it when my father died and then saved it and invested it, working minimum-wage jobs and living a minimum-wage life until I was old enough and wise enough to get higher-paying jobs, all the while investing the money well and allowing it to grow. I have worked my *ass* off to get where I am in life, and the only thing the money did was make up for the fact that I was an orphan and had no parents to use as a backup plan.

I want to say to these people: "I'll trade with you. You have *your* father die of cancer when you are fifteen years old, and you have *your* mother go missing and end up drowned in a hotel bathtub, and you get my finances. I'll rewind and keep my parents; you offer up yours." What do you think their response would be? And these are my supposed *friends*. People who are supposed to have my back. People who are supposed to cheer me on.

I have always felt terrible around these people. I loved them, but I would leave the interactions feeling wrong in some way. Smaller. Damaged. As if I did or said something wrong. I would review the time spent together and look for where I could have made a mistake. That fucking *sucks!* And I realize now that I was re-creating my relationship with my mother. A woman who loved me but also secretly hated me. A woman who was proud of me but was also always jealous of my youth and the beauty that came with youth.

It took me a *long* time to allow these friends to fade from my life. And when I did, I felt wrong. As if I was not being loyal. As if I was bad. As if I was too sensitive. It's not fair, and I feel so sad for the little girl in me that kept whispering, "I don't want to play with that lady. She makes me feel bad about myself." Or "She's mean to me."

What is it about wounded souls attracting wounded souls? Law of attraction, I suppose. Duh. But it fascinates me to look back at the stages I was at in my life and the people I attracted at each stage. And then how, as I outgrew them, as I evolved, I made myself wrong for the friendships no longer fitting. I scolded myself for not being loyal. But did *loyal* really mean "spending time with people who secretly envied me"? Did *loyal* really mean "hanging out with people who talked down to me"? I realize this with certainty: evolution is self-love. The more we evolve, the wiser we become and the more we learn to truly love ourselves. All the parts. Especially the wounded, seemingly broken bits. And the less we are willing to settle for scraps, for a mediocre life. The more we learn to love ourselves, the less we will tolerate working a job we hate, dating someone who doesn't adore us, living someplace crappy, jealous friends, and low-vibe conversations.

As I journeyed higher and higher up the mountain of self-love, I noticed that the friends I had who hated themselves no longer fit. They could not be happy for me when I succeeded. Instead, they were jealous. If I suggested that they, too, could live lives they love, they argued for their limitations, listed all the reasons this was not possible. In order to not make them jealous or feel less than, I made myself smaller every time I was around them. That is the part that felt like shit. That is the part that made my heart ache. It really was *me* making myself a shell, in order to not offend.

As I grew into my sense of self and as I grew into my truth, I began to realize if I am going to be real, live my true life, be my true self, and expand into my fullness, I *am going to offend* people. Some people will not like me. In fact, some people may hate me. And that has nothing to do with me. Or my self-worth. The same way some people curse the sun when it shines too brightly. (Yes, I just compared myself to the sun. How's that for learning to love myself?) But, seriously, the sun is just the sun. Some people love when she shines brightly; some people curse her and close the blinds. Imagine if she adjusted her display, trying to please everyone? *That* is what I used to do. Big, small, fun, serious, smart, dumb, slutty, refined . . . whatever the person or people near me needed, simply to be sure they would be comfortable. To not ruffle feathers. It was *soul killing*. And it attracted to me the wrong people.

It has been painful expanding into who I truly am, honoring my needs, and speaking my voice, because I had so many people in my life, on my email list, and following me on social media who, it turns out, were deeply offended by me being me, me speaking my truth. So I had to deal with that. It hurt. Ouch. With each one. Their words were so mean and so nasty. It hurt to be so grossly misunderstood. "I'm good," I wanted to explain to them. "I mean well. I only want to help. I just want to show you how magical life can be, that you don't have to live with so much fear and limitation, that your body can heal, that you can be or do or have anything you set your mind to."

But eventually the herd thinned. As Caroline Myss says in *Anatomy of the Spirit*, "Always, a shift in awareness includes a period of isolation and loneliness as one gets accustomed to the new level of truth. And then always, new companions are found." I was left with those who thrived when I thrived. Who got inspired as I achieved. Who applauded me for being raw in my writing and for having opinions that went against the norm. These people said, "Rock on, sister!" and "Amen!" and "The lion is roaring," and all of them said, "Do not stop." They did not say, "You live in a dream world." Or "You have this view because you have money." *Those* people have fallen from my life. And my heart broke with each one. There was a lot of self-doubt. It took a while, as most breakups do, for me to see how much I never really did fit with those "friends." I love them with all my heart. I always will. Love does not go away. But I need a tribe who supports me.

I know now, as Shaman Durek explains in *Spirit Hacking*, when people's energetic signatures are aligned, they "move at the same pace and in the same flow. They feel uplifted in each other's company, and their relating is always smooth." He continues with, "Then there are those people who drain us, and stress us out, and rub us the wrong way, and leave us feeling drained, or frazzled, or off balance—not because of anything they say or do, but because of the frequencies they generate. This is what happens when our signatures are misaligned." He finishes with, "A lot of relationship friction is a result of misaligned signatures. It's not that anyone is doing anything wrong, or that anyone is behaving in such a way that needs correcting. The discord is happening on much subtler and more fundamental energetic levels, which means that simple behavioral adjustments aren't going to shift them. We're not meant to be in relationship with everyone."

Life is so short. And relationships are *so extremely* important. We should not be afraid to shine brightly around our loved ones. We should not feel as if we have to hide our optimism or our thriving. We should not be forced to agree that "life is hard and everyone is susceptible to disease" when we know in our heart otherwise. We should not be afraid to expand our wings and take up space. We should not be afraid to be ourselves. And the *only* way we can find our tribe is by doing all of the above.

We were taught wrong, you see. We got it backward. We shrunk ourselves, and bent ourselves, and twisted ourselves into weird shapes to make the others happy. To make the masses happy. So then we felt alone. Because we knew if we became authentic we would alienate everyone. Alien. Alienate. We felt like aliens. And we felt like in the movie *Cocoon*, if someone saw us peel off the human suit and be our True-Self Light Beings, we would not only be made fun of; we might be killed. So we hid. And we felt alone. And we agreed with all the fear-based and lack-based, and scarcity-based, and disease-based paradigms. And life here was not very much fun. And we turned to addictions or medications. Or we isolated to avoid depressing low-vibe conversations. The solution is expanding those wings. Knocking down all the china. Wrecking everything in our life that is too small. Creating space to fully *be*. Singing with joy. Breathing fire. Melting. Melting. Melting all that does not fit. And then flying up to the top of the mountain where the other dragons await us.

PART 4

LOVE

The way you make love is
the way God will be with you.

—RUMI

CHAPTER 23

The Butcher

hooked up with a twenty-six-year-old butcher from Whole Foods. I'm forty-seven, by the way. He picked me up during lockdown. In fact, the grocery store was the only place you *could* pick someone up during lockdown. And I made out with him on the side of the road after our first date, a river date. In my bikini. With my car door hanging out in traffic. Smooching all over him for all the world to see. A world that was, at that time, standing six feet apart and wearing face masks and latex gloves. Take that, coronavirus.

Gunner was more than a twenty-six-year-old butcher at Whole Foods. He was so much more. And I saw that in him right away. And yet my mind scolded me—told me he was *way* too young and so totally not the guy I was looking for. Fortunately for me, and for him, I had just started rereading *The Surrender Experiment* by Michael Singer and had just—and I mean the-night-before just—decided I was going to stop waiting for life to unfold the way I had planned it to and to say yes to each thing the universe put in my path.

The universe put Gunner in my path less than twenty-four hours later. Tall, handsome, muscly, sexy, young, spirited, amazing, beautiful Gunner. Sexy—did I say sexy? I'm going to say it again: sexy, sexy, sexy, sexy, sexy. This guy was *so* sexy. And so puppy-dog young. And apparently extremely attracted to me.

I had turned down the double twenty-four-year-old ménage à trois. And in the eleven and a half months that had passed since then, I had been celibate. *Celibate.* Again! Because I had been sitting around waiting for Mr. Right. Who, apparently, was taking his sweet old time showing up in my life.

When Gunner appeared, I realized that maybe these young guys were manifesting for a reason. In the eight years since I had been so shattered in New York, I had not dated. I had barely interacted with men. I'd had one six-month romance with a man who showed up at my front door as my new property manager. ("Renee, you will never meet a man if you don't leave your house. You can't expect one to just show up at the door." "Yes, I can. If I am meant to meet one, Source will send him to my door the way she sent Pele . . .") But that romance had ended while I was on my book tour, over a year ago, right before I met Jonah, who I had turned down because he was "too young."

I could not help but notice that as soon as I vowed to say yes to what the universe was offering, another young man appeared. *Immediately.* Maybe the universe knew what she was doing. Maybe these young guys were stepping-stones on my way to the guy who would fit really well and stay awhile. Maybe I was *supposed* to be saying yes instead of getting up on my high horse and being all judgy and saying things like, "I could never be with a guy that young." Because you know what? I could be. And I was. And it was delicious.

But he had to talk me into it. He had to *persuade* me. He literally had to look me in the eyes and say, when I was trying to send him home after our second date, a hiking date, "Renee, you want me to go home because you are used to being alone. And cooking dinner alone this evening and going to bed alone is what would be comfortable for you. My being here is making you uncomfortable. Which is incredibly sexy, by the way. I want to worship your body. I want to massage you. I want to kiss you all over. I want to touch you. And I think you should let me. I think you should allow me to make you feel uncomfortable . . ."

Oh my God he was so right. And so confident! I should let him. I needed to let him. I had not been touched by a man in so long, I forgot what it felt like! My body was *craving* male touch. Craving kisses. Craving sex. Craving being held. But I was *so* nervous.

Shall I set the scene?

It's late afternoon on a weekend. We have just finished hiking, stopped in a café to eat, and returned to my home. We had discussed watching a movie and both decided to shower—separately. I have put on cozy clothing and returned to my living room to make a phone call. He walks upstairs from my guest bathroom and joins me on the sofa.

Gently, he begins to massage my feet. I instantly get *incredibly* nervous. I'm on the phone talking to my friend in the hospital, trying to figure out if I am driving to Denver and back the next day to visit him. Gunner, who is now smelling like soap and wearing a soft white bathrobe, *only* a soft white bathrobe, keeps massaging my feet.

I have to hang up, but I'm so scared of what's coming next. I can't believe I have forgotten so completely how to do this.

I hang up the phone and he leans in to kiss me. I recoil. I am so unbelievably nervous. He's too young. I'm so uncomfortable. I feel like I'm about to make out with a friend's *son*. He is completely right: his being here is making me *so incredibly* uncomfortable. And he calls me out on it. To which I respond, "I need wine."

"Okay, let's get you some wine," he says. With a big smile on his face and mischievous sparkles in those dreamy, big brown liquid eyes.

We walk into my kitchen, where I pull out a bottle of wine and hand him the bottle and the opener. He is standing next to me, well, *towering* over me, in my guest bathrobe. White terry cloth. Yummy. He is so close to me, the side of his body is touching mine. The top of my head is level with his shoulder. His biceps are the size of my thigh. His beautiful hands, the size of the wine bottle. He begins to open the wine.

"This is what I need," I say. "You standing next to me in a bathrobe opening a bottle of wine." I need it so badly. This type of energy. This type of electricity. The feeling that only being with a man I am sexually attracted to can produce.

We go back to my sofa. He starts to massage my feet again. Bathrobe. Naked underneath. Wine. Foot massage. Gorgeous, handsome, *huge* butcher from Whole Foods. I met him because he had seen me shopping, took his break, and was waiting for me in the lobby of the store as I left.

"Hi," he said to me.

"Hi," I responded.

"I'm Gunner," he said.

"I'm Renee," I said back.

"You are so beautiful. Are you single?" he asked.

I had just vowed to say yes.

"Yes," I responded.

"Can I get your phone number?" he asked next.

"Yes," I responded.

"Would you like to do something together soon?" he asked.

"Yes," I responded.

I had a moment where I floated above my body and watched. *Who* is *this woman?* I found myself thinking. *All she says is yes.*

He waits until I drink half the glass, and then he takes it from me and places it on the coffee table. He stands up, reaches for my hand, and pulls me up to standing, saying, "Now we are going to your bedroom." He leads me by the hand up the stairs, and then he picks me up and carries me to my bedroom. He carefully places me on the bed.

And this is where I flounder, again. I refuse to kiss him properly. Just small kisses with my lips only. No tongue. What the hell?

It's not like I've never kissed a man before. He finally says to me, "I want you to stick your tongue out. Just stick it out. Touch me with it." I start laughing. He starts laughing. But he's serious. This twenty-six-year-old is now teaching me how to kiss. Why am I so incredibly shut down?

"Seriously, just put your tongue out. I want to feel it." I keep laughing. I have majorly regressed in age. I have the giggles and can't stop. He finally gives up and starts undressing me. He removes my shirt and my bra. Begins kissing my breasts. Then my stomach, working his way down south. For a man so young, he clearly knows what he's doing. Meanwhile, I am completely fumbling this entire opportunity. I missed the slow, sexy, nervous, first kisses on the sofa. I missed the more intense, more passionate, deeper kisses in my bed. We have now progressed to my being naked and his head between my thighs. So, I decide I want to backtrack to kissing him properly. I say, "Come here . . ." and put my hands on his huge muscular shoulders. I want to kiss him for real. But he takes it as, *time for intercourse* . . . and says, "Are you ready for this?" We've had about five minutes of foreplay, but I am so nervous I am just fumbling left, right, and center. I say, "Should we get a condom?" As if I hadn't ruined it enough . . .

He says, "Condom? Do we need one? I don't have anything." Then he pauses. "Do you?" I get quiet. And then I drop the complete boner-killer bomb. After refusing to use my tongue when kissing him. After not engaging in any foreplay. After freezing like a young woman being touched by a man for the first time, I say, "I have herpes." I just blurt it right out there. *Splat!* Like vomit hitting the concrete.

What the *hell*?

Looking back on it I realize some part of me was trying to make myself as undesirable, as wounded, as broken, as diseased as possible. I realize now that I have been using this excuse to make myself undesirable since I got diagnosed seven years ago.

Bless his heart, he says, "Okay, let's get a condom." I start to overexplain: I have not had an outbreak for five years, and the outbreaks I had were so minor I could never tell if it was herpes or a spider bite. I'm ruining everything. I'm talking too much. And now I have planted a seed of fear. So the rest of the evening, while fun, is laced with fear. He keeps getting hard and then soft, hard and then soft, the condom keeps falling off. We go through an entire box. I begin to get chafed. We need lube, which sucks and becomes a sticky mess and basically means I'm no longer enjoying myself. And he ends up having to jerk himself off to have an orgasm because I'm so embarrassed by what's unfolding that I simply can no longer participate properly.

It's comical now, as I write this, but there are so many lessons in it for me.

The first and biggest one is this: I had been *so sure* of what my "perfect partner" was like that I was missing this *amazingly perfect* man who was *in my bed*! Source had supplied *exactly* what I needed. A *perfect match!* And I was missing it! Because of my preconceived ideas.

Second: because this man did not fit my idea of "my partner," not only was I missing it, but I was destroying the whole thing. I was nervous and insecure, and some part of me that is not authentic, some part of me that is people-pleasing and worried about what the world thinks of me, some part of me that was brainwashed in church and in the cult kept telling me he was "too young" and I was somehow "bad" for getting in this situation with him. So, instead of ravishing his body and allowing him to ravish mine, instead of rolling around in love and pleasure, instead of relishing in the touch of a man, leaning into the almost overwhelming feelings of nervousness, I shut down and botched the whole thing.

I realize now that feeling of chemistry with a man is incredibly overwhelming. Almost to the point of frying my circuits. But it also means I am alive. So alive. I never ever, *ever* want to shut down those feelings again. I turned to wine. Which helped. But I would rather sit there and feel all those feelings. I'd rather be able to say to him, "I am so overwhelmed by my attraction to you, by how

I feel, and I want to just sit here for a few moments and experience it. Feel my heart pound. Feel my mind freak out. I want to savor this." And then I would like to kiss him slowly and sensually and be nervous and *enjoy* being nervous. When I was younger, I'd always had to be drunk to initiate intimacy. It finally hit me that I no longer wanted to numb out overwhelming feelings in this way.

Third: I feel shame around my genitalia. I had no idea that I did, but I do. The herpes diagnosis made me feel like I could hurt someone, like I was diseased and unclean. When I think of that area of my body energetically, it is as if the energy is stuck there. Blocked. Like I am holding on to hurt and shame. And I realize somewhere along the line, sometime since the cult, repressed deep shame around that part of my body surfaced. It's like a dark black energy. Like tar. Like it *is* oozing with disease. As if the cells there are not pink, and pure, and thriving, and full of life force energy, but instead, clogged with gunk—filled with guilt, self-judgment, and deep shame.

I realized I did not need to mention condoms to Gunner. That I never need to do that again. I suddenly *clearly* saw how venereal disease *is* a dark current of shameful energy. It makes zero sense that two Light Beings coming together to share love and play and touch and passion could possibly spread disease in the process. It only makes sense that light and love would be passed between the two people. It only makes sense that the natural state of the parts of our bodies that create new life would be filled with light and with life and with a bright, pure love and magic, life-creating energy.

I realized that I was buying into an old church-induced fear-based, shame-based belief system and paradigm that no longer served me: one that said I had to protect myself from disease when I made love to someone. I had not realized I was still carrying such an outdated belief system. I had never even thought to analyze that belief system. So, I brought up the subject. It was my fault. I mentioned condoms, and then I dropped the herpes bomb. And in doing so I took young, sweet, sexy, pure, kind, light-filled Gunner out of his

paradigm of fun and love and passion and play and plopped him
into fear. Or planted a dark seed of fear in that fertile light-filled
mind. Which then lingered throughout our entire interlude.

I'm sure he went home and googled "herpes" and saw image
after image of people with their entire groin area covered in red,
weeping, puss-filled sores. Which is the exact dark, clogged,
disease-ridden energy of shame and sin that organized religion created around sex. Because, in the joy and pleasure and love and
union of sexual intercourse, humans connect with each other and
they connect with God. No church is needed. Sex with love is
direct connection to God/Goddess. Of course the church needed
to make it evil. To scare people. To create fear-based currents of
thought that manifested disease in the body. Anyone I have ever
talked to who has an STD got it because of some shame-filled
situation. I have never heard of a person getting one from an all-
love-based interlude. And I have also heard from friends who have
an STD that they have never passed it to a new partner when that
new partner is a love-based relationship. Both of these confirm my
belief that venereal disease is a manifestation of shame and guilt,
a dark current of energy passed in non-love-based intercourse.
Not because casual intercourse is wrong or bad, but because the
mind believes it is wrong or bad and creates disease as a form of
self-punishment.

Anyway, I ruined this opportunity. This magical gift from
God/Goddess. I shit all over it. I know my herpes is gone. I know
I can no longer give it to someone else. I know I got it because
my soul wanted me to stop overriding my Inner Guidance when
it came to men and sex. And to show me I still carried a shame-
based paradigm around sexual pleasure. I also realize this is why
my outbreaks were so mild. I *only* got an outbreak if/when I was
contemplating having sex with someone who would not have been
good for me when I was in such a fragile stage of psychological
healing. And each time it was two tiny, pinpoint, red bumps side
by side. Exactly like a spider bite. As small as humanly possible

to stop myself from having self-destructive sex. And also, a hint from my body that my mind was associating sex with shame and with something bad. Something wrong. I had picked that up from my mother and then the cult and then from my self-destructive romance in New York. That dark energy of shame around sex made its way into my body, into my second chakra, and in doing so manifested disease.

After this experience with Gunner I realized I no longer needed herpes. I no longer wanted to hold that confused energy in that glorious part of my body. I released it all. As I was taught to do by that doctor who helped me heal my hip, I thanked my body for the disease and I allowed it to go. I asked those cells to regenerate as thriving, light-filled, pink, perfect, luscious, passion-giving and -receiving cells. So that the next time they held parts of a male body, they wrapped those parts in love and light, in healing and in joy. This is what sexual intercourse is supposed to do.

So, yes, I blew it with Gunner. With the magical gift that he was. There was no fixing any of that. I'm sure he has always thought, *Sex with older women is supposed to be amazing.* And now he must think, *Sex with older women not only sucks, but exposes my young, healthy body to herpes and disease.* No fixing that, which is a shame. But I definitely learned what *not* to do the next time Source drops a gorgeous hunk of a man in my path.

CHAPTER 24

New Zealand

Lisa was a tall, beautiful, slim blond with one green eye and one blue. She had a toothpaste smile and stopped men dead in their tracks. Hired by the same photographer as I was to go on this around-the-world trip, Lisa became an instant friend.

Two days into our sea-kayaking adventure, Lisa paid $500 to get airlifted out by helicopter. We were twenty years old. It was 1993. $500 was *a lot* of money. That's how much it sucked.

But we had no idea. So, when the photographer suggested we all go on a five-day sea-kayaking adventure, we said *yes*. New Zealand had so far proven to be *spectacular*. In the South Island, we had explored the city of Queenstown, eating delicious food and going to the theater. We had signed up for the original AJ Hackett adventure: jet boating up the famous Kawarau River to bungee jump three hundred feet off a bridge and white-water raft down. We had purchased and lived in a maroon and yellow 1965 Commer camper van that overheated every time we went steeply uphill, leaving us to explore the area on foot until it cooled down.

And we saw more sheep than people as we drove over and through endless rolling hills of lush green covered in wildflowers.

On the North Island we hiked through rain forests to breathtakingly blue fjords, sparkling coves, and craters filled with turquoise water. I posed in a bikini on a coastal glacier moments before the top came crashing down. And when the photographer suggested sea kayaking up the coast, I imagined luxuriously soaking up sun on white-sand beaches after navigating through crystal-clear, calm, shallow seas.

We packed our gear, bought groceries, rented and loaded up the kayaks, and set off. We were heading north up the east coast of the North Island. The first day was windy, creating a choppy sea. And our route took us straight into the sun. For *hours*. It was a tough paddle over and through large swells, and by the time we made it to the beach, we were dehydrated, sunburned, hungry, and exhausted. Our eyes were fried. We all had headaches. Some were seasick. And we used all the energy we had left to pull the kayaks up onto the beach. Stumbling, we dragged them up past the high-tide line. And then we unloaded. We were *famished*.

Unscrewing the lid to the watertight compartment that lined our hull, my boyfriend Matt and I were hit with a very sobering reality: everything we'd packed was soaked. Our watertight compartment, we realized, was *not* watertight. And not only was everything soaked, but it reeked like (and in the case of our food, *tasted* like) fiberglass. Rendering most of what he had packed inedible. *Fuck!*

We laid our soaking-wet sleeping bags out to dry in what was left of the setting sun and set up our wet tents. We hung our wet clothing on tree branches. And we ate the small amount of soggy fiberglass-tasting food we could choke down. We slept hard and got up at sunrise for day two. It was no better than day one. Windy, choppy, huge ocean swells, and depleted bodies.

Three hours in Lisa called for evacuation. She spotted someone on a beach with a satellite phone and made a beeline. The waves were constantly crashing over our kayaks, pitching us sideways, soaking us. Matt and I saw Lisa turn, we saw the photographer follow her, and we decided right then to skip the second night without food and paddle all the way to a hotel—a journey that was supposed to take two more days—getting there as the sun set. We ate at the restaurant but spent the night in our tents on the beach. We could splurge for only one or the other: food or accommodation. Plus, all the other guests looked like normal people who had driven there in nice cars. We looked like people who had been shipwrecked and washed up on the beach.

We woke up the next day before sunrise and decided to head back. We couldn't afford three meals in that restaurant if we were going to keep traveling for five more months. We were going with the wind and the current, so it was faster; we were going away from the rising sun, so it was less blinding, and our bodies had been fortified by delicious food and a long night's rest. Plus, heading back felt *good*. As we neared our first camp late in the afternoon, we decided to keep going and try to make it all the way back.

With one crucial mistake: we had forgotten in the short time we had been on the North Island, after spending two weeks on the South Island, that we were farther north and the sun was setting a full hour earlier. About ninety minutes from our campsite, the twilight turned black. It got pitch-dark as we rounded the last point. We both stopped paddling and just sat in defeated silence for a spell. We were exhausted and out to sea in complete darkness.

And then I remembered, we had set off just before sunrise, and there had been a light at the end of a dock near our launch ramp. We could see it way off in the distance, and we aimed straight for it. One hour, two hours . . . we were *exhausted*. But it was getting closer. After midnight now. When, suddenly, up ahead was a crashing noise. Like water crashing on a beach. We slowed a bit. Could it be an exposed reef? We were still at least an hour's paddle from shore. Something began to glow in the darkness. Something white. We stopped rowing. We were gaining momentum. What was happening?

Wham! We got slammed onto dry sand. Oh. My. God. Low tide. *Extreme* low tide. It was a new moon. Now, instead of an hour's paddle, we had an hour's *walk*! Carrying that heavy-ass kayak with all the soaking-wet gear inside. Are you fucking kidding me? *After* three days' worth of paddling in one go! And we had no choice. To leave the kayak and all the gear would be to lose it when the tide came in. As a full-grown adult writing this, I would say, "Lose it. All of it. And buy more." But as a twenty-year-old traveling on a shoestring budget for six months, that was not an option.

We began walking. Him in front, me behind. Walk twenty steps, stop and rest. Walk twenty steps. Stop and rest. Walk to the other side of the kayak and pick it up with a different hand. Walk twenty steps. Stop and rest. For an hour and a half. This thing was so fucking heavy.

And then . . .

At 2:00 a.m. we made it to the light. We made it to the coast. But we had made it to a dock that was twelve feet above the sand and a boulder wall. No sign of the boat ramp. Pitch-black darkness. Two choices. One: start walking up and down the coast to find the boat ramp. Or, two, we heave this heavy-ass kayak up the boulder wall. It was angled. We could make it. We chose heave. And up we went. Crawl up a few boulders, heave. Crawl up a few more. Heave. Crawl up some more, heave. And then we dumped it. On the side of the road. We had made it this far. We absolutely could not carry it one inch farther. It was close to 3:00 a.m. And that thing was heavy as fuck. The chances of it being stolen in a town that had more sheep than people seemed small enough to risk leaving it there. We walked the fifteen minutes back to our youth hostel and passed out. Our kayak was still on the side of the road when we got back there at noon the next day.

CHAPTER 25

ROMEO

I wish I could be the woman who could have a part-time lover. One who randomly showed back up in my life every few months. A friend with benefits. But I am not this woman. I get attached. *Quickly.* As I mentioned before, I am famous for turning every guy I hook up with into my "soul mate" before I know anything about him. Well, before I know anything besides: (1) he's hot, and (2) he's fun.

I have a cricket in my bathroom. Most people would kill it or put it outside. But not me. I turned it into my pet. His name is Cricket, and I greet him every time I see him the way one would greet a pet cat or dog. I leave out little dishes of water for him and I ask him how his day is. I tell him "sweet dreams" before I go to bed. I get excited when I see him in my bathroom or in my closet, and I worry that I will step on him when I get out of bed in the dark. I will cry when this cricket dies, and I will miss him.

I had a gecko in my studio apartment in Hawaii. His name was Fred. And I even had a centipede for a day. I learned the hard way with that one: centipedes, like spiders, are not pets. When you see them in your bedroom, kill them. I woke up in the middle of the night to a fiery pain in my inner thigh and that thing *latched* on to my soft skin. I had to *yank* if off me and throw it into the wall, and then I got a fever and aches all over, sore throat. Centipedes are not pets.

I even had a chipmunk living under my oven. Pele brought it inside and it escaped. Once it was hiding under the oven, it would not come out. So, I scooted a small bowl of water under the oven, with a little plate of banana bites and cut-up almonds. In the mornings I would make my breakfast, Pele's breakfast, and a tiny mini-plated chipmunk breakfast. It took me a few days before I realized that the chipmunk had shelter, food, and water and would never leave. In fact, it was shitting and pissing all over the floor under my oven and would never leave. By the way, this also happens to me with houseguests. They don't shit and piss all over my floor, but they never want to leave.

My plants are my babies. When my orchids start to bud, if the buds dry up and fall off before they bloom, usually because I got excited and, in my effort to make sure they have everything they need to bloom, overwater them, I cry. *Cry.* Every time.

And don't even get me started on Romeo.

Oh, see, you got me started . . .

Romeo is a male deer—the *world's most handsome male deer*—who showed up one day outside my office window. He was walking down the path between my trees when I noticed him. He must have felt me looking, because he stopped and turned his head. Then he saw me and approached the window. He looked into my eyes and I told him, with my eyes and my mind, that I loved him and would not hurt him. Yes, I already loved him. I told you, I get attached quickly.

He then began pawing at the mulch outside my window and lay down. He spent the entire day dozing, licking himself, scratching a bit. He left at sunset. And he came back almost every day for two months. I got to watch him grow up. I saw him shed coats, from golden brown to gray. His antlers went from small and velvety to large and velvety, to extra large and hard, to super sharp and pointy. He would put his nose up against my windows and look for me. If he did not find me in the office, he would look for me in the kitchen. I kept his nose prints on the windows. I loved them. I loved him. And when he left in September, I cried. I missed him so much, it hurt. And it took me two weeks to stop looking for him outside every day.

Nine months later I finally asked my landscapers to remulch his sleeping spot. The bare spot he had left made me sad, it made me miss him, and it was not visually appealing. The following week a crew showed up to install new mulch. And that afternoon—I am not kidding—Romeo showed up. Talk about an Aspen buck. I guess he needed his bed remade. He wanted his Frette linens and was not coming back until he had them.

He stood in the window until I noticed him, nose pressed against the glass. And once I saw him and cried out with joy and welcome, he settled down in his spot and fell deeply asleep. He was much skinnier, and his antlers were tiny. He was so skinny, I was worried he was sick. After a long day of deep sleep, he left at sunset. For a month. I became worried I would not see him again, that he really *was* sick. So I told myself he had stopped by to say hello after a long migration and was now up in the mountains gaining weight. Which he was! He returned the day before my birthday. He was fatter. And his antlers had grown. He stood and stared at me with those massive gorgeous deep brown eyes. So full of love. So wise. He communicated so much love through those incredible eyes, and then he settled down to nap. He came back daily for a month. He's famous on my social media.

The wild thing is this: the day Gunner came over to hike, Romeo met us at the front door. Gunner, six foot three and all muscle, said he felt afraid, because Romeo was so big. I told him Romeo would never hurt him, and I moved myself between the two of them. Romeo nibbled on some tree leaves and walked toward my driveway. He was back in his spot when we got home from hiking. But the next morning Romeo bucked my window. For the first time ever. I thought maybe he had caught his reflection in the window, but that had never happened before. Then he stationed himself outside my bedroom in the flower bed. I had never seen him lie down outside my bedroom. He spent the morning there. And then after only a few more visits, he left. The final time I saw him, he was napping outside my office window, and there was another young buck on the path. They both left midmorning, and Juliet (a doe who visits me) arrived that evening. Nose pressed against the glass, looking for me.

The following day two fawns arrived, no mother in sight. And that afternoon the young buck reappeared. This time with an antler damaged—broken and hanging. He settled, skittishly, in Romeo's spot. He saw me look at him as I walked past the window and got startled, then ran away. I can't help but wonder about the significance of the young buck in Romeo's spot and the parallel of Gunner in my home, in my bed, but just for a moment. I kept thinking how weird it felt to see the young buck in Romeo's spot. How, even though I was thrilled to have him there, something felt wrong. And he felt it, too, the young buck. Something told him he didn't belong there. He settled down for just a moment and then ran off. The young buck . . . in Romeo's spot.

CHAPTER 26

PƏNƏMƏ

The best way to deal with being marooned in a hidden bay in the middle of nowhere in Panama while a troop of Panamanian military men wearing bulletproof vests and holding machine guns keeps you captive on the bow of the yacht owned by some stranger you just met who happens to have no papers for his vessel and never told the Coast Guard you were traveling with him . . . is to ask them to take you wake surfing behind their recently confiscated Colombian drug-running boat.

In crocodile-infested water.

That's what I did.

And it worked.

Yes, they almost ripped my arms out of my sockets when starting the four *enormous* engines. Yes, they kept their machine guns slung across their chests the entire time. And, yes, the water really *was* full of crocodiles.

But it did get me out of that situation, got me cooled off, and got me released back to my hotel that afternoon while almost everyone else spent a week in that god-forsaken spot waiting for help from the US government.

It started with a harmless surf trip to Panama. I arrived at the airport in Panama City, and Hugo picked me up, along with some weird dorky kid he had met in Montana, or Costa Rica . . . or maybe some kid from Montana he had met in Costa Rica. I don't know. But the kid—young man, really—was scared. He had never traveled before and was carrying a down jacket in the heat of the tropics . . .

We drove a long way on pothole-filled dirt roads that were not much more than hacked clearings through a deep, dense, lush, tropical jungle. We all took turns driving, and Dan, who had never driven on dirt roads, kept hitting the potholes too fast, then slamming on the brakes, causing all of our surfboards on the roof to lurch forward, threatening to project nose-first off the top of the car and making Hugo and me worried about popping a tire in the middle of the jungle. Hugo was a philanderer who had no respect for women, but underneath it all he had a good heart and he was actually really funny. People loved him. Ladies loved him. In fact, I had loved him (as was my way back then) for about three minutes doggy style in my old bedroom while visiting my mother for Christmas six months prior to our trip . . .

It was, needless to say, a supreme disappointment (as non-loving sex is if we are truly honest with ourselves) and was never repeated again. It also was, not surprisingly, brought up multiple times in arguments brought on by the long hot car ride over impossible dirt roads. He, to his credit, owned up to his poor lovemaking and blatant disrespect for women. I think he blamed it on his upbringing. I can't remember. "You're right. I'm a pig. I should date strippers and eighteen-year-olds, not women, but I had to at least *try* for you. Can you blame me?" he said, to my surprise. I laughed. And once we got it out in the open, the tension dissolved, and he was a really fun traveling companion. Why he allowed the dorky kid to tag along with us, I do not know, but he had a soft heart in that way and probably wanted to save that kid from a month in Costa Rica wearing a down parka and getting beaten up by mean surfers.

At one point on the drive, I spotted a guava tree and asked Hugo to stop the car. I got out and grabbed some guavas, taking a bite out of one. As soon as I felt it on my tongue, I spit my mouthful into the dirt; it was filled with maggots. "What the hell?" Hugo and Dan asked at the same time, their windows down, looking at me standing beside the car with spit on my lip. I showed them the remaining piece of guava, with the maggots. And *Dan* threw up! Not me, Dan! This was my traveling crew . . .

After a full day on the road, covered in sweat and mosquito bites and caked in dust, we checked into a rustic hotel room at Santa Catalina and paddled out for a sunset surf, surfing what turned out to be one of the best waves of my life. It was a right point break, and the warm green ocean was as smooth as glass, reflecting soft fluffy clouds turned pink and orange by the setting sun. The waves were a few feet overhead, and the surfers were all paddling energetically, competing for the best position. They seemed to not mind a bikini-clad woman entering the mix, but they weren't that excited about Hugo, and they definitely didn't like Dan, with his pasty white skin and matching white boxer shorts sticking out of his surf trunks. Dan, fortunately, had no idea where to sit in a surf lineup and paddled so far outside, he might have been scouting for whales, which, as luck would have it, kept him safely away from the waves and out of earshot of cruel comments.

We spent a few days there, surfing as long as our bodies would allow and resting in hammocks to recharge. We ate three meals a day at the large community tables at the hotel restaurant and got to know some of the other guests in and out of the water. The local surfers were aggressive, and after a few days of paddle battles in the water, Hugo and I began talking about maybe moving on.

That evening, after surfing, Hugo came back to the hotel room with the following story. "I met this guy at the bar. He's an ex-pat living in Costa Rica, and he has an eighty-foot trimaran anchored off the coast here. Because of his visa, he has to stay out of Costa Rica for a month, so I asked him, if we pay for fuel, would he take us up and down the coast, looking for surf? In fact, I talked to three other guys, and they're willing to go in on it with us . . . We could leave tomorrow."

I answered with a definite "Yes!" We left the following morning, dorky Montana Dan in tow. For two days we looked for surf. Dan got seasick immediately and never got better, so after making fun of him for a while, we dropped him off on a tiny island and left him there all day while we surfed. The surf was small, and no matter how far up the coast we went, we found only tiny waves. Dan finally left his island and paddled—*paddled*—to meet us. Why we were so mean and didn't pick him up, I have no idea . . . I used to be a bit of a narcissist. (That is why being shattered by life really did heal me. That story is told in *The Burn Zone*.)

I remember someone had a guitar. While living in Hawaii, I had learned how to play two songs on a guitar: Bob Marley's "Redemption Song" and a Spanish guitar rhythm. After a few beers one night, I grabbed the guitar and boasted to the small crowd that I could play anything they requested. We sat grouped on the deck, under a dark star-filled sky, a warm breeze giving us a break from the heat. The boat rocked slightly and pivoted occasionally, tethered to its anchor at the bottom of the sea. In the few days together, we had become a family, and I felt comfortable with these men.

"'Redemption Song,'" someone cried out. What were the chances? I started to play. And they were impressed. And they never knew I couldn't play anything else because someone else wanted to show off his talents on the guitar, so I graciously obliged.

The next day we got pulled over. A fierce-looking white cigarette boat with four *enormous* engines and a crew full of bulletproof-vest-wearing, machine-gun-holding Panamanian militia appeared out of nowhere and pulled alongside us, then boarded us. Then told us we had to follow them because, apparently, the captain of our boat had no papers. Not only did he not have papers, but he had not called any of us in as his passengers. *And*, out of all the passengers, I was the only one who had my passport with me. Not even Hugo, the self-proclaimed "world traveler," had his passport with him.

We followed the military vessel, with one of the men on board, and all of us on the bow, with a machine gun pointed in our faces, to a small hidden lagoon tucked way back in the trees, seemingly in the middle of nowhere. Out of sight completely from any boats navigating along the coast. And there we sat. On the bow, in the sun, for hours. *Hours.* While the head honcho went to talk to his boss. We realized quickly that they were trying to find a way— any way—to confiscate the boat. The one they were on—the one with the huge fancy engines—was recently confiscated from Colombian drug runners. We found this out when Hugo finally convinced our guards to drink a cold beer. And another one. And another one.

Hugo is from Ecuador, so his Spanish is flawless and filled with perfect street slang, and as I said before, people loved him. "Come on, you guys, it's so hot. You know you want a cold beer. No one will know. We won't tell El Jefe. Relax with us. Have a beer." He got them drinking, then laughing, then joking . . . and finally started bragging about my surfing ability. "In fact," he said, "she can surf behind your boat."

"En serio?" they responded. They did not believe a girl could surf, especially behind that boat. "Sí," he replied. "She's really good. In fact," he said, "she'll do it, in a bikini, if you let us go, like, let us go back to our hotel today . . ."

The captain of our trimaran and the other surfers looked on with complete amusement. Amusement at Hugo joking with these guys holding machine guns and amusement that I was even contemplating letting them take me wake surfing behind that powerhouse of a boat with those four massive engines. I was craving surf. We had found so little. And I was melting in that heat. I really *wanted* to go wake surf behind that boat. I didn't know about the crocodiles . . .

"Bueno," the guys said. "Okay." We had a deal. They jumped on the boat. Bulletproof vests, guns slung across their shoulders, dressed in all black. Boss Man had been gone for hours at this point. The chances of him returning anytime soon, they knew, were too small to worry about. I sat on the swim platform of the trimaran, in my smallest bikini. They threw a line over the back of their boat, between the four engines. I had insisted Hugo go with them. (There was no way I was letting three machine-gun-carrying, bullet-proof-vest-wearing Panamanian whoever-they-were pull me off alone into the lagoon and who-knows-how-far-away from the rest of my friends.) So Hugo, God bless him, jumped in the boat with them. They took off at full throttle. Almost pulled my arms out of my sockets. I had to let go of the rope so they didn't. They had no idea how to drive a boat for a wake surfer. Hugo told them, "Despacio and suavemente." (Slowly and smoothly.) They tried again. And I got up. And they cheered. And I surfed. But they got too excited and revved the engine, so I let go of the line in order to save my shoulders. And I sank slowly into the warm nebulous green water, sitting and straddling my board as my momentum died, and I patiently waited for them to come back and get me. The trimaran wasn't that far away. I could still see the details on the faces of my friends watching me from the stern of the boat. The white trimaran looked beautiful floating on the green water, surrounded by the thick green of the jungle. I had a moment of utter joy as I took in the spectacular scenery.

The military boat came back quickly. "Loca!" they yelled. "Estás loca!" they all said on top of each other as they rushed around to get me. I smiled, thinking they were impressed with my wake-surfing skills. I had *no* idea that the water was filled with saltwater crocodiles. They thought I knew; thought I just didn't care. Thought I was sitting there cool as a cucumber, simply waiting in crocodile-infested water like I had all the time in the world for them to come get me . . .

I had *no* idea about the crocs until they picked me up and Hugo told me. By then we had won their trust and their respect.

They let us go, Hugo and me. We gathered our stuff from the boat and walked to the main road, then took a bus back to Santa Catalina. The others stayed. For a week, I think. By then Hugo and I were long gone. He to Bocas del Toro and me to my safe little home in Florida. Both of us filled with joy from our adventure with our divinely appointed gun-slinging friends.

CHAPTER 27

RELATIONSHIPS

Being in a romantic relationship is so interesting. It truly brings up all our stuff. All our defense mechanisms. All our triggers. All our walls. And only when we are centered in who we truly are, only when we have our own back and love and respect and cherish and nurture ourselves the way we wish others would, are we truly ready to be in a romantic relationship that empowers both people through the long haul.

Before that we don't have much to give. We are really just looking to take. We are wanting to be saved, rescued. Men, too. Before we truly love ourselves and the lives we have created, we are expecting the other to fill a void, and we get terribly disappointed and feel incredibly wounded when that person does not. Which always happens. Because the other person *cannot*. We have to do that ourselves. But, also, being in a relationship before we are truly ready does help bring all these wounds and insecurities to the surface. And if we are strong enough to not blame the other, if we are aware enough to notice the patterns and stop saying, "I just need a different partner. This one is not right for me . . ." intimate relationships are the perfect environment to see the wounded parts of us that need healing.

One of the reasons I joined the cult is because I was dating the most wonderful, most compatible man I had ever met. And after a few short months, I found myself criticizing him inside my mind. Then it slowly started to come out my mouth. (This was my pattern with *every* man I had ever dated.) I had always reasoned with myself, *This is the wrong guy for me. We have to break up.* And I would find a new one. Only to have the same pattern appear. *When I find the right guy, I won't be so critical,* I would think to myself. But here I was with the right guy. Someone so nice and so kind and so smart and so sexy, and here I was doing the same thing. This was when I realized the problem was not with the men in my life; it was inside me. Something was lacking inside me. Something was broken inside me. My need to criticize others had to come from a place of criticizing, not being happy with, myself. I broke up with the guy. I told him I loved him too much to treat him badly and that he deserved someone who could treat him better. I also told him I was breaking up with him for God. I'm not kidding, I really did say that. Who says something like that? Oh yeah, someone in a cult. And then I submerged myself full force into that cult, because I wanted to fix whatever was broken inside of me. We all know where *that* led.

But, on the other side of all this, I have two bits of wisdom to impart. Two things were happening with my relationships: One, yes, I was unhappy inside myself, did not love myself, did not nurture myself, and was looking for safety and love and protection and validation outside myself. Which, as I mentioned above, never works. We must learn to fill those needs from within if we ever want to be truly happy and at peace. Otherwise we are forever anxious that the person or the people we believe are supplying those feelings will leave.

Second, I had never picked the right man. Because I did not know who I was, because I was not vibrating from a place of wholeness and thriving, I was attracting kind, fun, sexy, wonderful men, but also men who matched this immature needy me: men who were not truly whole and thriving. Some part of them was wounded and lacking and looking for a woman to fill the void. Do you see how this gets two codependent people leaning on each other, using each other as Band-Aids?

I really think most men need to discover who they are and how they fit into the world before they can be great partners. Otherwise, there is a part of them that is always distracted. A part of them is unavailable, unsettled. I think only when a man knows who he is and where he fits in the world can he relax, breathe deeply, stop trying so hard, and be fully present with his partner. This is just an observation. I have never actually dated one of these men.

Most women, on the other hand, seem to not feel completely settled, safe, and secure in this world until they have a man. Again, just an observation. But I notice female friends of mine who settle much more into a grounded sense of self when they have a man in their lives. Even the women who claim they don't need a man or aren't looking. Yes, I have some incredibly independent female friends who really *don't* need a man in their lives, but they are only a very small select few.

It seems men need to feel needed and women need to feel desirable. It's a shame we think we need to be other than how we are to be loved. I wish I could tell men, now that I am grounded in who I am and feel whole on my own, "I just need male energy. I need your strong arms around me. I need your kisses and your whiskers against my face. I need your testosterone and your sense of male groundedness." I don't think men understand that we women often just need their male energy to balance us out, that men, just being men, add so much to our lives. That they don't need to own mansions and yachts and planes to be worthy of our love. Which makes me realize that it's time for us women to realize men need our feminine energy, our softness, to balance them. That they don't need us to look like supermodels. They don't need us to be a size

6 or look ten years younger; they just need our feminine essence, which we all have naturally. I smile as I write this because I realize on a deeper level how much we *all* need each other, how much we complement each other, and how we don't need to be "more productive" or "prettier" or "wealthier" to be lovable, to be worthy of love.

I think about how what I needed from my parents when I was young were cuddles, kind words, supporting words, undivided attention at times, embraces. Not my mother's beauty or my father's work ethic. Those things, as a matter of fact, often distracted them from giving me kind words and undivided attention. I realize the greatest gifts we can give to one another are these simple things. These things we are born with. Not anything we have to go out and get or achieve.

I think so much sadness in the world stems from so many of us feeling like we have to prove our worth. Like we are unlovable just the way we are, so we have to achieve to be worthy. When we are babies, we intuitively get that we brighten up the room just by being ourselves. We intuitively get that we deserve to be loved and taken care of. We intuitively get that we need to do nothing more than sit and watch and coo and breathe to be worthy, to change the vibration of a room and everyone in it. Have you noticed when a baby gets carried into a waiting room or onto a subway car? All the tired faces start to relax and open. All the lifeless eyes start to sparkle. The cares and concerns drop from bodies as each person focuses on the baby. All babies have to do is sit and be themselves and they uplift the vibration of the planet person by person with each interaction. They return hearts and minds to love. We can do this, too. We *did* this once. We were born to do this. It just gets trained out of us at an early age.

And then, instead of being the love that we are and attracting love from all over, we decide we are unlovable and we become desperate to "find love" or "find a lover" so that we are not so empty and alone. We dissociate love from sex, and in our confusion many of us go out into the world looking for sex. Thinking that will help fill the void. But, as the saying goes, we can never get enough of what we don't really need. So the constant need for distraction becomes unquenchable.

If we want to be able to date freely and love different people, we have to approach dating from a place of wholeness. From a place of loving ourselves and loving our lives and engaging with romantic partners because it adds fun and pleasure, not because we are weak and broken and needy and believe that only a romantic partner can fix/save us. Don't you see how that gets us hooked? And gets us devastated when it does not work out? And attracts the wrong people? Don't you see how that makes us undesirable? And needy? And powerless?

Men can sense that desperation. The same way we sense desperation in men. It's a turn-off. No one wants to be the reason for someone else's happiness. It's too much pressure. And it's an impossible void to fill. Most men seek freedom. Most women seek safety. If we women can learn to have our own back, to not betray ourselves in order to people-please, to give ourselves what we are wanting from men, we give ourselves safety. The anxiety goes away. We know that no matter how unpredictable other humans are, we can *always* count on ourselves.

Then, when we engage with men, we do so for pleasure. We do so because life is so much more fun with men in our lives. We do so because we love being held by and nurtured by and protected by men. Men love to protect and provide for us. They do. They feel their best when they are doing this for women they love. So, we mustn't overcorrect and build ourselves so "strong" that we "don't need men." I was guilty of this, too.

Once I healed I felt as if "needing" a man made me weak. I was confused and thought that if I was whole I did not need a man to complete me. But then I saw a video from a dating "expert" who mentioned, "Men need women and women need men." He then corrected himself and said that two people who are whole do not "need" each other, but that life is so much more fun for men with women around and vice versa. Something about that line truly struck me. I want fun. I want play. I want passion. I want to be naked on my back with my legs apart and have a strong, handsome, sexy, masculine man on top of and inside me. I love that feeling. It is a feeling that *nothing else in life* can give me.

I'm tired of pretending I don't want it or that wanting it is bad or makes me weak. I still have a block here somewhere. A block that whispers quietly, "Well, only with the *right* man." Who is the right man? I have been waiting my whole life for the right man. Since I joined the cult I have been missing so many hot, fun, sexy, kind amazing "wrong" men. What if the man the universe is placing in my path, the one I am mind-numbingly attracted to, is the *right* man? I mean, he is. Of course he is. He is the right man for right now. He is the stepping-stone. He *is* the right man for right now. Otherwise he would not have been placed in my path. He is not a "temptation." He is not God testing me. He is the *yes* on the way to the next *yes* on the way to the next *yes*. Otherwise there is no growth. There is no experience. There is no learning. Fucking hell I have missed so many fun times with so many sexy, amazing men in the last eight years because I kept waiting for the right man. Head smacking emoji here. And in doing so, I have missed the growth opportunities and the *fun!*

I think, as Abraham-Hicks says, "We are always getting ready to be ready to be ready to be ready." They also say we won't be impatient if we are enjoying the journey. Sitting at home celibate and touch deprived for years while waiting for Mr. Right to show up at my front door is *not* enjoying the journey. Going out into the world and meeting lots of interesting, fun, kind, handsome men *is*.

CHAPTER 28

Dis-ease

I eventually heard from Gunner. He was afraid of herpes. He said he wanted to see me again, but he was freaked out. And he asked me to go get tested to find out if I really had herpes. Which I decided to do. Because I wanted to know. So I made the appointment to go get tested. And when I explained to my doctor what I wanted, she told me my last blood test showed antibodies to herpes and that getting tested again would be a waste of money.

"Showed antibodies to herpes" is different from "having herpes." I heard that and thought, *If my last test showed antibodies, that would mean my body had encountered the disease and developed a way to fight it.* I wondered why the last time I had a test she had said, "You have herpes."

I asked her to please just go ahead and test me for everything. A full exam and a full STD blood panel. I told her that maybe my last test was a false positive (because I knew if I told her I was sure my body had cleared the virus, she would tell me that's not possible). Best just to leave that out of the conversation.

The idea that our body cannot rid itself of a virus or a disease makes zero sense. If our cells are constantly replenishing themselves, why would anything "last forever" or "not go away"? That belief system is illogical. The reason something stays is because of the mind. I love Western medicine for emergencies, but I hate it when doctors proclaim voodoo curses: "You will have this forever." I'm serious. Many doctors unintentionally curse their patients, planting in their fertile minds dark seeds of "no healing possible" that become realities. If you don't believe me, read Dr. Joe Dispenza's *You Are the Placebo.* Or Dr. David Hawkins's *Letting Go.* Or Caroline Myss's *Anatomy of the Spirit.* Or Anita Moorjani's *Dying to Be Me.* Once I removed the shame-based, fear-based thought streams around my genitalia and the dis-ease there, I removed the dark energy and allowed the healing light to flow. And my blood test showed the change.

My results came back: all normal, all healthy. No trace of herpes. My dis-ease returned to ease, the natural state of our bodies.

So, um . . . not only have I been basically avoiding sex for eight years because of it, but I have also been telling every guy I get naked with that I have it. Which, let's just say, lowers their enthusiasm a tad. *Plus,* I published in *The Burn Zone* that I had it. I might as well have been rolling down the window at stoplights and yelling to strange men, "I have herpes! You don't want to have sex with me. Don't come near me. You do *not* want me!"

Okay, it's funny. And it served a *magnificent* purpose. Because it showed me how diseased and undesirable I thought I was. It showed me that I still carried those thoughts implanted in me by my mother and the cult. I had been using herpes as a way to shun intimacy. I kept making myself "not good enough." Well, I'm done with that.

It was only after Gunner, and when I suggested using a condom, that I saw what I had been doing. How I had never questioned what I had been taught as a teenager about sex and sexually transmitted disease and condoms. How I had just innocently bought the paradigm that I had to have my man wrap his penis in latex if I was going to have sex with him. What a weird concept. It feels *terrible*. "Let's get as close as our two bodies possibly can, but let's wrap your body part in latex so we don't really touch." What the hell? Who thought of that? And how had that been okay for me so much of my life? How had I never questioned it before Gunner?

Only after this experience with Gunner was I 100 percent sure my body would rid itself of dis-ease in that area. I imagined the dark, stuck energy flowing away. I thanked herpes for being in my life and for keeping me safe and for showing me what I had needed to learn: that I was making myself undesirable and diseased to keep men away. Because I was afraid. Because I was afraid they wouldn't like me or would see me as unlovable. Because I was afraid I would give too much of myself and lose myself again. Or—I realized there was some of this still buried in me—maybe they *would* like me at first, but then discover over time that I was deeply flawed. Whatever the reasons, I was okay now on my own, but I was still afraid of getting close to a man. I had fought so hard to regain my sense of self, my sense of balance, and I was terrified of becoming undone the second I got into a romantic relationship.

It was only after Gunner that, like with my *Burn Zone* book publishing process, I finally decided to accept myself exactly as I am. I finally said, "Enough! I don't care if he doesn't like me. I don't care if he's freaked out about herpes. I am *magnificent*. I am kind and loving and fun and interesting and beautiful. I am magical and unique. And if he can't see it, there are many out there who can." I lifted and shifted. And with that came a bright sparkling energy into my womb and genitalia. I imagined all my cells turning pink and pulsing with life. I imagined those parts of my body embracing a male's genitalia and spreading only life and love and healing life force energy. And I knew the herpes was gone. I knew it, in my bones. And yet I no longer cared. Because I also knew that with the right man or men, it would not matter.

CHAPTER 29

CAN YOU DANCE?

And three weeks later in walks Milo. Who had read *The Burn Zone*. Who knew about the herpes. And who absolutely did not care.

Gorgeous: tall (six foot three); huge kind, sparkling blue eyes; and a lion's mane of soft, curly golden hair that cascades down his back and smells like heaven. He is so kind, and so smart, and so sweet, and so sexy. His body is all muscle, and his smile is all white teeth and bright light. He's limber and he's lithe. He's my surfer neighbor, and he's thirty-three. Fourteen years younger than I am.

For this reason he is "not in my dating pool." Because I still have not grasped the fact that younger men *do* find women my age attractive, I just assume a man that age would never be attracted to me. And yet there are sparks. I can feel them. Every time we talk, we resonate on a deep level. We have known each other in past lives. I get glimpses of them when we talk. All the way from the times of Atlantis.

My friends ask about him and I say, "Not yet." And I mostly say, "No, not ever." Because he is my neighbor. And he is too young. But then he moves away. To a beach town farther north, and suddenly he's no longer my neighbor. Suddenly he becomes more romantically viable. Because if it gets awkward, there is now space. Because we both know we are not permanent partners. The age difference is too much. And he wants to get married and have kids. I don't. I'm forty-seven. And even if I weren't forty-seven, I don't believe in marriage and have never wanted kids. It could be fun, but it wouldn't last. Could be fun, wouldn't last. Could ruin a friendship, but could be worth the risk. Why does love and lust have to be so complicated?

After a drunken night, we end up in bed together and it is magical. Comfortable. Scary. Fun. We're both nervous. And excited. And worried. And content. I learned so much from the Gunner experience that I allow myself to relax into and fully enjoy this one. Milo feels like home to me. I feel so safe with him. I absolutely love lying in his arms. I absolutely love kissing him. And I love the way he feels on top of, underneath, and inside me. I simply cannot believe we waited so long to try this. And I am so proud of us for saying yes.

I have known him for close to two years and would not have said yes anytime sooner. For multiple reasons. But my yes streak has opened my eyes. It's changed my world. Reading *The Surrender Experiment* and then *Year of Yes* (by Shonda Rhimes) has shown me that when we say no to what the universe presents to us because it does not fit our "plan," we do ourselves an incredible disservice. We miss magic and miracles, and we miss necessary growth. If I had not said yes to Gunner, I would not have been so willing to say yes to Milo.

I finally knew for sure that in my effort to wait for Mr. Right, I was missing crucial steps I needed to take in order to get there. I realized the universe kept trying to offer me these magnificent men, and because they were so young, because they did not fit into my idea of Mr. Right, of who and what I was looking for, I kept saying no. Which was leading me nowhere except lonely nights and touch-deprived, sex-deprived boredom. I realized I was getting absolutely nowhere in my search for Mr. Right.

As soon as I told the universe I was open and would say yes, Gunner appeared and movement began to happen. Fun began to happen. Love and play and flirting and sex and romance began to happen. A drizzle of rain began healing the barren, scorched, parched desert of my body, mind, and soul. I kept thinking I was a strong, independent woman and did not need a man. But that dating expert was right: life is so much more fun *with* men in it, need or not. I realized how ready I was to have men back in my life. And how much I had been depriving myself of a very necessary part of being alive by convincing myself I could live without them.

There is a certain spot that men fill in a woman's life. A certain energy they ignite. Passion, sexuality, vibrancy. We open and we glow when we are around a man we find attractive. We beam light and the nozzle to our Kundalini energy gets opened to full force. When we feel safe with a man, we bloom. I'm not sure anything else in life creates *this* type of energy awakening for us, nothing else besides the presence of a man we find attractive. Depriving ourselves of this feeling, depriving the world of this light, just because we are "strong independent women" and don't "need" a man, feels injurious to ourselves and to the world. Maybe this need gets replaced by something else as we get older and wiser. I don't know. But at this stage in my life, it is long past time for me to admit that I *do* need men. Heterosexual women need men. Or some of us need men. *I* need men. I'm done lying to myself and the world; I'm done acting as if I don't.

Gunner did not last. He was a one-night romance with six months of cat-and-mouse. But he started the flow. He opened my mind and my dating pool. Suddenly any age was an option. Suddenly any career was an option. Suddenly all I needed was kindness and attraction.

In paddles Milo. With his longboard and his golden hair. The night he slept over, he looked like Jesus. After a dinner filled with friends, dancing, and tequila, we ended up skinny-dipping in the ocean, romping naked down a wide-open, low-tide beach under stars and moon. Our walk home was barefoot and in towels. Milo looked like Jesus to me. The bare feet. The tall body. The long hair and the beard. The towel robe. His energy is saint-like, as well. Always has been. In my drunken, happy blur, he was Jesus. And I was his Mary.

My heart already loved him. It has for lifetimes. So it only made sense that my body would, as well. And when we fell asleep together, I was on my side, wrapped up in his arms. I don't sleep well next to others. I'm too energetically sensitive. And many people are fitful, loud sleepers. But not Milo. He sleeps peacefully, quietly, as I knew he would. And I slept well next to him. Loved having him in my bed. Wanted him to never leave.

The thing is this: we did not last. We had only one more night together. Because, according to him, we're "not a match." But what is a match?

This is what I am realizing. This is what I have finally discovered, after a lifetime of searching: we are longing for connection with Source/God/Goddess. We think it's another person, but it is not. In our desperation to find someone "until death do us part," we do not realize that we are wanting to partner with the Beloved. Our Creator. As much as we love connection to each other, we really are looking for our connection to Source. We get confused when we hand that responsibility and that power over to another.

And so here is the epiphany: *each* person we encounter is Source/God/Goddess animating a human form. When we say no to someone who has been placed in our path, because they don't fit our checklist, we miss a *crucial* step in our own growth and evolution. Yes, maybe we do have a destined soul mate. Maybe we are meant to partner for life with a certain someone. But often we are not yet ready for that partnership. We have not done the work, not had enough growth. We discover so much about ourselves when we are in a romantic partnership. Often the people we pass up while waiting for Mr. or Ms. Right are the *exact* steps we need, the exact lessons we need to learn, in order to become a match for Mr. or Ms. Right. We are missing very important steps when we do not follow this attraction.

When someone lights up to us, we must explore. When we feel love and attraction, we must follow it.

As Kahlil Gibran says in his beautiful book *The Prophet*:
When love beckons to you, follow him,
Though his ways are hard and steep.
And when his wings enfold you yield to him,
Though the sword hidden among his pinions may wound you.
And when he speaks to you believe in him,
Though his voice may shatter your dreams as the north wind lays waste the garden.

So Milo told me he didn't want to see me again because "our sex was fleeting" and I "did not align with his goals." But how can he reach his goals without taking the necessary steps to get there? What he does not realize is this: I am a necessary step. He can have me *and* his future wife. In fact, he needs me, he needs to *enjoy* me, in order to become the man who is ready for his wife. Don't you see how wonderful that is? Don't you see how fun? He gets both. He should have both. And maybe even a few more other fun, sexy, kind, amazing steps along the way. There does not have to be intense pain when we are aligned. Love does not have to be entwined with hurt, with fear, with pain. If we are awake and honest with ourselves and with each other, we can tell when the energy of partnership has faded, when it is time to move on. It may be sad, and it may take time to fill the hole the person left in our routine, but because we are balanced and awake, we will survive it. Because we understand divine choreography and are now open to partners the universe picks for us, we *know* another lover is on her/ his way. When our partner is the Beloved, we know he is always there, and the next form to love will appear. This, at least, is what I believe.

Rumi writes, in his beautiful poem "Community of the Spirit," "You moan, 'But she left me.' 'He left me.' Twenty more will come. Be empty of worrying. Think of who created thought. Why do you stay in prison when the door is so wide open?"

Why *do* we stay in prison when the door is so wide open? Milo said he was feeling vulnerable—he was setting himself up to get hurt—so he did not want to get emotionally attached. But I believe we *must* get emotionally attached to each other. Actually, I would like to get rid of the word "attached" and replace it with the word "intimate." We must be emotionally intimate with our lovers. As with anything we do in life, we must go all in. If we want to do it well, we must do it with all our being. Body, mind, and spirit.

I once went to a talk given by a highly pedigreed Caucasian psychotherapist. Harvard, Yale, honors, you name it. And he told the story of his pedigree, which was clearly meant to impress but instead bored me. And turned me off. But he got my attention when he spoke of his first residency out of Harvard. He said he went to a Native American reservation to "help them." He went to the mental hospital. And his first patient was an elderly man. And in my mind I instantly pictured a tribal elder. As he introduced himself to this man, he went through his long list of schooling and achievements, all of his awards. To which the man politely listened. When the doctor was done with his soliloquy, this patient looked at him with kind, wise eyes and asked him one thing:

"Can you dance?"

It brings tears to my eyes.

This young doctor was caught off guard and simply replied, "What?"

To which the elder repeated himself, a bit louder, "Can you dance?"

The young doctor replied, "Sir, I do not understand . . ."

"If you cannot dance," the Elder said, "how can you heal?"

I began to cry when I heard this. It resonated on such a *deep* level to me. It is such a simple thing but is so *incredibly* profound. As all deep truths are.

How can we heal ourselves or anyone else if we cannot dance? If we do not allow ourselves to dance? To be goofy, to be wrong, to be expressive, to be free? To figure it out as we go, to make mistakes? To flow with ease, with grace? To allow the life force energy to move us as she will?

Fortunately this young doctor was awake enough and wise enough to realize he had landed at the bedside of his next teacher, of his *real* teacher. And he stayed on that reservation for ten years studying shamanism. His main takeaway was this: Our heart knows the way. When the thoughts of the mind are not in alignment with the *knowing* of the heart, there is imbalance and mental agitation. When the words that come out of the mouth are not in alignment with the thoughts of the mind and the knowing of the heart, there is imbalance and mental agitation. When the actions of the body are not in alignment with the heart and mind, there is imbalance and mental agitation. And when there is too much misalignment of heart, mind, words, and action for too long, there is mental illness. Only when heart, mind, and action are aligned is there wholeness, integrity. And only when there is integrity is the soul at peace. We will never be at peace inside our mind if we are ignoring the Knowing inside our heart. When our soul calls us to walk in a certain direction, we must go or we will suffer.

How can we possibly make love with another and not love him/her with our heart and mind, with our words? If we are honest with ourselves, if we are awake and aware and present, if we are not shutting our spirit out of our body, we cannot. So, yes, dear Milo, we will become emotionally intimate when we are physically intimate. It is as it should be. My heart, my mind, and my body wide open to you. Isn't that what we are all craving? That level of safety? That level of connection? What if we knew ourselves well enough, loved ourselves well enough, to allow ourselves that connection with more than the elusive Mr. or Ms. Right? What if we allowed ourselves that level of bliss and joy and affection with each stepping-stone on the way to Mr. or Ms. Right? We would live *now*. We would love *now*. We would expand and grow deeper. We would create beautiful love-filled, passion-filled memories that would never go away. We would learn to love completely and without fear because we would be able to *practice* doing it. With each stepping-stone-magical-love-affair placed in our path. And when it was time to say goodbye, we would have no regrets. We would have only wisdom, and joy, and wonderful memories, and love.

Soldiers have a saying, "The only way out is through." I believe it applies to all walks of life, and especially to love. When we try to close the door on a romantic relationship that has not run its course, in an effort to "not get hurt," we cause ourselves unbearable suffering. Because our soul knows the lessons have not yet been learned. Our heart says, "I want to love this person, explore this person" and the mind says, "I want to shut the door on all these overwhelming and uncontrollable feelings, and I'm going to because I don't want to get hurt." Our energy is split. Half wants to walk away, is trying to walk away; and the other half is staying, is clinging, because it knows it is not done. The only way out is through. Go all in. Go for it. Balls to the wall. Go big or go home. Whatever your favorite war cry is. All in. Heart wide open. Body, too. All in, my love. As long as the divine makes it last. And then, when the energy begins to shift or fade and the pulling away starts, both partners let go. This is the ride of life. This is the ultimate thrill. Surfing at its finest. Ride the wave when the energy is there and kick out when you hit the shore. It's obvious if we pay attention. And it's not crushingly painful if we both let go when the time comes.

I once heard a spiritual teacher say, "Change is not painful; resistance to change is." As we become masters of life, we tune more and more into the energy flow. Then we are never alone.

Because that energy is Source. We are following the flow of Source. And when it is no longer animating a partnership, when the energy shifts and fades, it is always and only because that energy is now about to flow through someone or something else. Another more aligned relationship or creative endeavor is calling. Or the energy is now being called back within for a period of soul growth. When both partners are awake, they can cheer each other toward the next step. Love each other, walk together, and when the time comes, lovingly let go.

CHAPTER 30

Same Woman

I have been in Argentina two weeks and finally acknowledged I need a new place to live; the apartment I rented is in a building undergoing construction, and the noise is way too loud. This morning I walked *far* to see the location of a place I had found online. It was way too far, but I kept going, thinking, *It has to be close. I just want to see*. I walked for twenty minutes. And then decided to turn back. It was too far on the outskirts, not a safe place to be. As I turned around, I passed a woman. She reminded me of someone I knew from Aspen, so I looked at her closely. Then I continued on. I returned to my neighborhood and walked into a café I had never noticed. I'm *hungry* and I want to write.

Just now. Close to two hours later. The door to the café opened, I looked up, and the *same* woman just walked in. What are the chances? I am more than a twenty-minute walk from where I saw her. I am on completely different streets, obvio (that's Castellano slang for "obvious"). There are literally *hundreds* of cafés between where I saw her and where I am now. I have never been to this café before. And she just walked through the front door. And she did it while I am still here! I have been here for close to ninety minutes.

I was in California a few months ago, and I went to Target. I parked quite far away, in the back corner of the parking lot, so as not to get stuck in the traffic jam and chaos of looking for parking spots near the entrance. A car parked next to mine and a couple got out. I noticed them because they were fighting. They followed me into Target. I spent maybe fifteen minutes inside, and as I walked out, I noticed they were directly in front of me. We had parked in the same place and walked in and out at the same time. Interesting.

Then, again, about two hours later, after I had done other errands, I decided to go eat on my way home. I chose a restaurant by the coast, about a fifteen-minute drive from Target. As I was finishing my dinner, the *same* couple walked in. What are the chances? Again, that they picked the same restaurant and that they chose it while I was still there? And that I was seated in a place to notice them walk in?

My point is this: we try so hard, those of us who are dating or looking for a romantic partner, to find someone. We go places we don't want to go. We force ourselves out at night. Maybe we look online. We struggle. "Dating is hard," we say. "Finding the right person is hard." So much effort. So much mental agitation. And Source just places people in our path. Again and again if need be. If this same woman can cross my path twice in one day, or this same couple, why couldn't the same man? The perfect man? Why couldn't God/Goddess place him on my path? And if I don't feel like rushing him, if I feel shy and not sure of approaching, why couldn't God/Goddess place him on my path again? She can. She will. And She will soon.

CHAPTER 31

GiViNG AWAy OUR POWeR

There is all this talk about giving our power away. People say it all the time. "Don't give your power away," or, "You gave away your power." I was saying it over and over as I traveled around doing my book tour: "I gave my power away when I was in the cult." "Anytime you let anyone else tell you who you are, you hand them your power."

But I still wasn't exactly aware of how often it happens, how insidious it is, or what it really meant. I mean, how does one quantify losing power? I figured it out on the plane ride to my final TV interview, when that hot young tennis player, the gift from the Book Tour Gods, sat next to me.

I had been relaxed, content, absorbed in my book. The plane door was about to close; the seat next to me was empty. I had done my last public speaking event the night before and had only one TV interview left. I was at peace. When suddenly a figure appeared next to me, breathless. I looked over as he sat down and swiftly went from at ease to uncomfortable. We started talking, and I worried about what I was saying, what I was wearing. Did I have food in my teeth? Did I look sweaty and tired? All of a sudden what this stranger thought of me became important. Because he was handsome.

But I heard a small voice inside my heart whisper, "*Don't* give him your power." And I got it. In that instant. It was lovely to talk to him and I enjoyed his company, but in that instant I made what I thought of myself the only thing that mattered. And with that decision, I took my power back. I went from feeling anxious and insecure and small to confident and secure and expanded and calm. Funny thing is: he clearly found me more attractive once I did that. His actions showed me.

Giving away my power means caring what someone else thinks of me. Period. Anytime I care what someone else thinks of me, I hand that person my power. I basically say, "You decide if I'm attractive. And let me know. You decide if I'm worthy. You decide if I'm likable or lovable. You decide if I'm good enough, funny enough, smart enough, sexy enough. You decide if I'm a nice person. You decide if I'm a good writer. You decide . . ."

Isn't that ridiculous? That I do that? That we all do that? That in subtle ways we do that all the time? That we allow strangers to decide whether we're being appropriate or if we're worth getting to know? That we allow strangers to decide whether we're attractive? That we care so much what other people think of us? That we allow people on social media to decide whether what we posted is "likable"? It's ridiculous!

It makes sense, in a way. As children we learned immediately that our survival depended on being liked and loved and included. If we were not, we would be abandoned and would die. But, unfortunately, it became so ingrained in all of us that as adults we don't realize how often we do it. We overstretch in yoga class to appear more flexible to strangers. WTF?! We lift too much weight in the gym to appear stronger to strangers. We women wear shoes that hurt and *deform* our feet in order to appear sexier to strangers.

We order food we don't want to eat or drinks we don't really want to drink. On and on it goes. I'm laughing out loud as I write this. It's ludicrous, and yet we do it all the time.

I know it seems like a minor detail, but to me it's huge. Writing and publishing *The Burn Zone* taught me so much. It taught me I have to believe in myself. It taught me I have to trust my voice. It taught me I have to trust my way of doing things when I am offering my divine gifts to the world, and I have to have my own back all the time; I need really strong boundaries. And even with all the wisdom and all the strength gained, I was still giving my power away each time I worried what the audience thought of my talk or I wondered if I wrote the right thing in someone's book. I even worried that what I posted on social media was not right in some way. I couldn't figure out why I left so many of my talks feeling drained, and then it all hit me on that plane ride home: Anytime we worry what someone else thinks of us, we are handing them the ability to decide for us who and how we are. It's not okay, and it needs to stop. Let's make a supreme effort together to notice each time we do it.

The biggest, most dangerous loss of power happens in toxic relationships. We accidentally get so wrapped up in being loved or liked that, in our effort to be approved of, we change up who we are so radically we become practically unable to find our way back. Loss of power manifests as loss of energy and loss of clarity. We actually wrap the filaments of our energetic body around the person we are trying to please, in an effort to control how they view us. In doing so we *feed* them with our life force energy. It transfers from us to them. How creepy is that? When this happens we become very unbalanced. We can't think clearly. We lose the energy to make changes, and we lose the clarity we need—about ourselves, about our path, about our worthiness—to leave such a dangerous situation. We lose the ability to make the right choices for ourselves. We stop listening to our Inner Guidance. We stop trusting it. And we defer to them. We make ourselves wrong. We use them as the weapon with which to flog ourselves, and we do so repeatedly until we are broken. The self-doubt sets in and the volume on it gets turned up to *max*. And in our effort to feel better, we cling to the person or situation that is draining us—which causes us even more confusion, more depression, more anxiety, less and less clarity, less and less energy. The mind starts running in circles, grasping for clarity, but the vibration is too low to find it. And in this discomfort we reach for action of some sort that will make us feel better, but we are acting from a place of confusion, so we make bad choices and end up in social situations or romantic situations or work situations that make us feel worse and even more powerless. It becomes a downward spiral.

We have to make what we think of ourselves *more* important than what anyone else thinks. Always. And forever. This is the self-love piece.

I have been reading Dr. David Hawkins's *Letting Go: The Pathway to Surrender*, and he mentions that everything has an energy signature. And that we get to choose if we want to align with that energetic signature or not. He explains how when we pick highly vibrating energies with which to align, we raise our vibration. With each word, each thought, and each action we get to choose: *align with love and truth* or *align with falsehood, grief, apathy, despair, anger*. As we choose higher vibrations in each moment, we become people we truly love. And once we love who we are, it is so much easier to not give a rat's ass (is that an expression? It makes me laugh) what anyone else thinks. And then we are free.

PART 5

WHOLE

Be really whole and
all things will come to you.

—LAO-TZU

CHAPTER 32

HOLDEN

I dated Jack Reacher for seven years. You know, the fictional character created by Lee Child. Six feet five inches tall, two hundred and fifty pounds, ex-military police? His body described as a condom stuffed with walnuts? Yes, that man. He was my boyfriend. In my head. For close to seven years. Until I ran out of Reacher books. But then decided to start reading them over.

I'm tiny. Size XS. And yet for the last seven years I always imagined being with a big, muscle-bound, tattooed ex-soldier, and preferably ex–military police. Why? Not sure. Maybe it was all Jack Reacher. Or maybe it was past-life stuff. Or maybe being the daughter of a World War II vet. But something about the warrior soul profile with the *huge* heart and kind eyes melts me. My father was a warrior with a huge heart. He was gentle, quiet, and kind. He was generous, patient, funny, and full of love. He was also intense, serious, and stern. Maybe I always wanted a man like him back in my life. Actually, not maybe, *definitely.* I definitely wanted a man like my father back in my life.

But I gave up. Completely. Just before Holden appeared.

Wait, I have to backtrack . . .

In February, a friend, Carrie, moved into my house. She had just broken up with her boyfriend and needed a place to stay. She also needed to create a whole new life, since she had moved to Aspen just to be with him. So, she created a vision board. And on her board she put an image of a handsome cowboy. I wanted one. And a shortcut vision board. So I asked if I could put the handsome cowboy on the screen saver of my phone. And pretend mine was the twin brother. She said yes, and so my relationship with Hot Stock Photo Cowboy began. For not very long. Because he wasn't my man. My man, I told Carrie, was a veteran, a warrior, and he was muscly with tattoos. In fact, he had been appearing in my home in visions. When I was decorating my Christmas tree, he appeared next to me, hanging ornaments. For just a flash. He had a dark beard and brown eyes. And lots and lots of muscles. He had a smile that lit up his whole face and a warmth that made everyone in the room feel safe when he was there. His huge, beautiful heart shined through his eyes.

He appeared in my kitchen one day, in a flash, cooking for me. And he appeared in my bed, with glasses, reading. I could never see his hair. And I could not tell his height. But I asked Carrie to find me a different image. "My guy is an ex-soldier, muscly, with tattoos. Can you find me one of those?" She looked. And sent me images. The men were handsome and sexy, but none of them was my guy. I tried using one as a screen saver on my phone, but every time I looked at him, I felt off. He lasted just a few days. Carrie, on the other hand, replaced Hot Stock Photo Cowboy with Sexy Muscly Tattooed Patriot. She claimed as her own one of the images she had found for me (which I didn't mind because she had given me Hot Stock Photo Cowboy Twin and, you know, soul sisters roll like that).

We were talking about Sexy Muscly Tattooed Patriot one night (yes, we were talking about the image on her phone as if he were her boyfriend. Do not judge us for having fantasies), and I looked more closely at the image, because on the man's left arm there was a photographer's website overlaying the photo, in tiny hard-to-read print. The photo was very artistic. I got the impulse to look up the photographer. Because the words were difficult to decipher, I had a few attempts before I eventually found the right website. And then decided to go to the photographer's Instagram page. I scrolled through the gallery. Lots of handsome, fit, shirtless men. I decided to look for a man who looked more like my vision.

The men were nice to look at, but it was overwhelming after a few minutes. Many of them were too defined. Zero body fat. Not very natural looking. And while those with more body fat looked better to me, none of them had the Light I was looking for. Not one of them had the right eyes. I can tell a lot by looking at a photo: how sensitive someone is, how kind, how caring, how open. And my heart simply could not handle one more cruel, self-absorbed, or emotionally unavailable man. No matter how handsome he was. Not even as wallpaper on my phone. I was about to give up, but I scrolled just a little lower and found the guy. The photo was *exactly* the vision I had of my man decorating my tree. Brown beard, brown eyes, beanie, T-shirt, and hoodie. Pensive. And yet his Divine Masculine qualities were there. I could see them in his eyes. I took a screenshot of the photo, trimmed the edges, and made it the wallpaper on my phone. For less than a day.

The thing with the guy on my phone was: every time I looked at him, it reminded me of what was missing in my life. And it made me sad instead of happy. My life was so good. Finally. I had found myself, I had figured myself out (more or less), and I was content. I loved my friends. I loved my home. I loved writing. I loved where I lived. The only thing missing was a male partner, and I noticed that I was becoming one of those women who was obsessing about having one. It was making me miserable. Focusing on the one thing I didn't have, instead of all I *did* have, was making me miserable. So I took him off my phone.

I forgot to tell you that after I took a screenshot of the photo, I clicked on the model's Instagram tag. It led me to his page, and I saw that he was a veteran living in Japan. He was also a *romance novel cover model!* I looked at the top few rows of photos and decided immediately that he was married. Or gay. I'm sorry to say it and I'm totally stereotyping, but men that handsome are either married or gay, or assholes. I forgot about the Light in his eyes. I forgot about his Divine Masculine qualities. This guy was, after all, just a stand-in image for my partner. I didn't need to know more about the real person. He was hot. He was romance-novel famous. He lived on the other side of the world. But his image would do. It was a perfect replica of my vision. I closed my phone. And used his image as wallpaper.

My life moved on. I traveled a bit. I snowboarded a lot. I secretly hoped my man was going to appear soon, and as soon as I acknowledged the thought, I let it go. Part of me had really given up hope.

The visions of him had started the previous year, in March. And they were so clear and so intense that on impulse I had ordered him a bathrobe. I chose a Japanese company and a robe called Men's Zen. The color was black, the material thin and soft, and I picked extra large for the size. I hung it in the back of my closet and kept the tag attached. I had almost forgotten it was there.

But close to a year later, the man had not arrived. The man was clearly not coming. I was delusional. I had met a lot of potentials. My energy was open. I slept with some of them. I smooched a bunch of them. But after my interlude with Milo, when it came to moving forward with the men I met, I could not. None of them was my guy. None of them matched my vision. Apparently my time enjoying stepping-stones had screeched to a halt. No matter how much tequila I drank, I could not make myself be with a man who was not my guy. In fact, I even told one of them: "I remember my partner from past lives. And he's on his way to me. I can't be with anyone who is not him . . ." The guy actually handled hearing that well. "You're *sure* I'm not him?" he asked. We both laughed.

Which reminds me: I forgot to tell you this part. The first time I took a karate class, I had a flashback of a Japanese past life. And the first time I held a katana (Japanese sword), I had a flashback of jumping through fire in war, as a Samurai. A female Samurai. With a male partner in battle by my side.

When the visions of the dark bearded man began, I was also getting visions of kneeling over my Japanese partner as he died on the ground near his horse, in a battle scene. In my vision the war had just ended. We had won. It was over. And he was killed as we were leaving. I was furious with God. And confused. I had not expected to lose him then. And as I held his hands and wept over him, I knew we would be together again, but that I would have to endure a long lifetime without him. We were both quite young.

When Romeo appeared in my window, I realized he had been my horse in that life. And I wondered if his appearance at my house was preparing me for my reunion with my partner. I had bouts of optimism—*my partner is coming.* And bouts of pessimism—*I'm delusional. No one from a past life is coming.* And yet I could not bring myself to be with other men. I tried. With Gunner. And with Milo. I tried to talk myself into being open to dating. But deep down I knew these men were not my divine partner. And interestingly enough, both men felt it and left almost as soon as they arrived. This is a tricky place in which to be. Part of me was so *sure* my lover from my past lives was showing up soon. And part of me was absolutely sure I was delusional. It felt like hell. Like I was stuck in hell. Like maybe I had severely screwed up my romantic karma and was destined to always feel as if the man in my bed was not the right man. I had learned all those lessons with Gunner and Milo. I had opened and I had grown. I had softened into saying yes to the men who appeared. And yet somehow there was always a quiet voice deep inside, whispering, "Your true partner is on his way."

One morning, at one of my lowest, most lonely, most if-I-don't-have-my-male-partner-in-my-life-soon-I-no-longer-want-to-be-here-on-this-planet moments, I was sitting outside on my patio having coffee when Romeo's antlers appeared in the trees over the far love seat. His head then popped up behind it, and he casually walked across my patio, less than two feet from where I sat. Other than the time he met Gunner and me at my front door, he had never been this close to me without a glass window between us. He looked at me for a moment, and then kept walking, to the back of the house and around to his favorite spot by my office. And I knew, *If Source can send Romeo to my patio while I am having coffee, Source can and will send my partner to me when the time is right.*

But the time never seemed to be right. I was forty-seven years old. When was he going to appear? When I was eighty?

As I mentioned previously, a girlfriend suggested I read *Letting Go* by Dr. David Hawkins. I read it cover to cover in just a few days. I started to practice the letting-go technique; I knew it would change my life. I finished the book and started reading it again. I focused on the part that said desire is a blocking of energy, that it sends the vibration into the universe of "I do not have." I worked on letting go of desire. I worked on letting go of my fear, anxiety, self-doubt, and sadness. I worked on letting go of my self-worth issues. I thought I had healed all this crap, but as I practiced this technique, I realized I still had more to heal. I did as Dr. Hawkins instructed me to, and every time I felt uncomfortable at all, I stopped, and I tuned in to exactly what the feeling was that I was feeling, what the emotion was. I did not push it away or make it wrong or try to change it. I simply felt it until the energy behind it dissipated. Results were immediate.

But at times I forgot about letting go. So I read the book again. Case studies documented women meeting men a week after starting the technique. Case studies documented people finding dream jobs or getting promoted shortly after starting to practice the technique. Medical issues and illness disappearing. Relationship problems gone. Drastic life improvement after drastic life improvement. I kept practicing.

And then I fell hiking. And got whiplash and a concussion. And got off social media. I believe everything happens for a reason, and that fall was so incongruous for me. I'm not clumsy. I don't fall. The spikes on my left shoe got caught in the shoelaces of my right and launched me face-first onto the hard snow-packed trail. I began to cry. And then got up. And then asked myself what I was being shown. The answer was that I was *still* way too concerned with what everyone else was doing and with what everyone else thought of me. *Still!* Fucking hell! I was also too focused on wanting a man in my life and kept falling into a victim mindset around not having one. *Still!* I couldn't believe all that crap was still swirling inside me.

I decided it was time to get off social media and go within. To read more, write more, and socialize less. So I did. For over a week. But an *incredibly* strong impulse to get back on Instagram hit me after I'd finished meditating one morning. And I knew, because the impulse came when I was in a high, clear, joyful state of mind, that I needed to follow it. So, I reloaded Instagram to my phone. And then I went to search for a friend's post. On the search page was . . . my vision board guy. The guy in Japan. I had basically forgotten about him. I hadn't been following him. I had removed him from my phone. Why was he appearing in my "reels" today? I tapped his photo, causing his page to open . . . to a post that he was in Glenwood Springs. Jaw drop. *Glenwood Springs?* A tiny, nondescript, old and somewhat run-down town forty-five minutes from where I live. It's where the closest Target is to me. It's fifteen minutes from Whole Foods.

Okay, so not only was it *totally crazy* that he showed up on my search page that day, two months after I had looked at his photos. But it was *absolutely* crazy that he was in Glenwood Springs. No one goes to Glenwood Springs. It's not a destination. It's a pass-through town on your way to the famous ski mountains. It's my pass-through town on my way to the freeway. Source had sent *my* Vision Board Man from *Japan* to *Glenwood Springs*! Not just a man who looked like my Vision Board Man. The *exact* man! And then Source had found a way to pop him into my Instagram feed and *make sure* that I see him! She literally (yes, Source is a she, sometimes a he, depending on my mood) *slammed* into my attention to get back on Instagram and search for a friend. And then she shoved him in my face. Goose bumps!

I had to reach out to him . . .

Didn't I?

I mean, yes, I had to . . .

Right?

How could I *not*?

Again, totally *not* like me, but I commented on his post. "Come to Aspen." He had close to eighteen thousand followers. The chances of him seeing my comment were minimal. I closed my phone and went snowboarding. Done. Message sent.

The next morning I checked Instagram again. He popped up at the top of my feed again. And he had posted again. Another post about snowboarding in Glenwood Springs, alone, having the time of his life, on that tiny crappy mountain. (Sorry, mountain, you are not crappy. But compared to Snowmass and Aspen, well . . .)

I commented again. I *had* to.

"Seriously. Come to Aspen. We're fun," I wrote. Closed my phone. Went snowboarding.

This time I thought about him when I was on the chairlift. Half of me really wanted to meet him, and the other half was completely afraid. After all, I had looked at some of his gallery back in January and decided he was married, gay, or a jerk. (Way to take yourself out of the game, Renee. Put bright, shiny, interesting, sexy, handsome, kind-looking men in the "not for me" category. Nice.)

By the time I got home from snowboarding, he had direct-messaged me. I was thoroughly surprised. He asked about getting lift tickets for Snowmass and Aspen. He had been told he had to preorder them because of COVID. We messaged back and forth, and by the following morning we had made a plan for me to go visit him in Glenwood Springs and go to the hot springs. I had never been. I'm telling you: people don't go to Glenwood Springs. Even though I had lived forty-five minutes away for over eight years, I had never been to the hot springs there. The hot springs in Glenwood were piped into a gigantic swimming pool, and every time I drove by them on the way to the freeway, I saw too many people stuffed together in one giant pool. It looked gross. (I realize I just contradicted myself. If no one goes to Glenwood, why are there so many people in the pool? I have no answer to that. I mean, apparently *some* people go to Glenwood. Just no one I know. We call it Glenweird.)

But, for this guy, I would *gladly* go take a bath with all those strangers. No problem. None whatsoever. I was already packing my bikini.

I was nervous driving there. Shaking and trembling and freezing cold with sweaty armpits. You would think I had never met a man before. I stopped on my way for a cheeseburger and ice cream. I didn't want to show up shaky and hungry. He called me after my burger. It was the first time we had spoken. He had a Southern accent and spoke with lots of Southern slang. He called me *darlin'* and told me he was "cutting" in order to prepare for a photo shoot the next weekend. He said his calorie count was way down, and he was a little spacey from snowboarding and weight-lifting on so few calories. I told him I had been a professional dancer and that I understood how badly one can feel when pushing the body like that while not feeding it properly. I asked if he would rather not have a visitor. He said, "No, I want to meet you. I think we have a lot to discuss." And he suggested I meet him in his hotel room. He would leave the door open. Because he was going to take a shower.

Um . . . wait, what?

I'm supposed to walk into a stranger's hotel room and do what? Sit on the bed while he's in the shower? And wait for him to come out? That seems awkward. And maybe not safe. He was hot. And he had kind eyes. And a kind voice. And he seemed to be well known. But I wasn't that sure about the "I'll be in the shower" scenario that was happening. I decided to drive slowly. I mean, how long can a shower take?

CHAPTER 33

TiGeR

When *does* the self-doubt stop? When do we finally decide to just trust ourselves? I mean, we've made it this far in life. Isn't it time to just trust ourselves? Trust our feelings and our gut instincts? Say no when something doesn't feel right and follow the energy with a "yes, yes, yes" when it does? Without having to analyze it a zillion different ways and call ten friends to talk it out?

What's the worst that can happen? You end up in a failed marriage or a financially devastating business venture . . . or brainwashed in a cult? I mean, that's not *horrible*. That's survivable. Right? For those of us who said yes to something similar and are reading this right now, we've survived. And I have to believe that if we had followed our gut instinct, we would have said no a lot sooner.

I have a friend who stopped loving and dating fifteen years ago. She gave up on it and closed her heart. And I simply cannot imagine life that way. Even after all the heartache I've endured. I believe the heart is like a muscle and needs to open and close, and then open wider, and then close, and then open wider and then close, in order to get stronger. Too many healers have proven that when we close our heart for too long, disease sets in. We have to learn to keep opening it.

We can never truly know what's in store for us. We do not have a crystal ball. And I have to believe that if we don't know what is coming next, it is because we are not meant to know what's coming next, that it would ruin the surprise. That we're supposed to have faith, faith that something bigger and larger than ourselves has our back and is sending everything our soul desires our way. All we can do is take the next step that feels right, that feels thrilling. And trust. Ignore the voice of self-doubt and keep walking forward.

When I lived in New York, I went to see the play *Bengal Tiger at the Baghdad Zoo*, about a tiger that haunts the streets of present-day Baghdad, seeking the meaning of life. Robin Williams played the tiger, and he was *magnificent*. In the beginning of the play, he is caged and gets shot and killed by the friend of a soldier who reaches his arm into the cage to harass him. He spends the rest of the play as a ghost, watching the idiocy of the war, witnessing the waste of the slaughter, contemplating life and death, and wondering if he's the devil because he always preyed on the small and the weak—creating a type of hell in his mind as he condemns himself, judging himself as evil, wicked, and the worst in the pile; sobbing and apologizing to God for being such a sinner. And then, one day, in his utter despair, he has an epiphany. He looks up and screams to the heavens, screams to God: "YOU KNEW I WAS A TIGER WHEN YOU MADE ME, MOTHERFUCKER!" And he surrenders. He accepts himself for who and what he is, accepts himself for all he has done and lived, and he is at peace.

Can we do this? For those of us who have worked on ourselves for years, for decades, trying to make ourselves better? Trying to be perfect? Trying to change and change and change? Can we not stop, finally, and accept ourselves? For those of us who have made mistakes, have messed up royally, can we not forgive ourselves and move on, wiser? Nicer? Calmer? With a hell of a story to share?

Jail. Addiction. Divorce. Infidelity. Financial ruin. Whatever it is that we did so horribly wrong, can we shine love on the dark spots of shame? Pull them up from the depths of our being and finally, once and for all, set them free? For those of us who have been betrayed and broken by people who should have loved and protected and cherished us, can we not forgive? Can we not take these wounds and learn and grow and blossom from them? Use all that we've been through to go out into the world and help others overcome something similar? When do we drop the pain of the past and blossom in the now?

We do when we decide to.

I have a thangka of a Buddha on my wall. I love thangkas. And I notice, in all of them, that the Buddha sits serenely in the middle, unmoving, and there is always a cloud of chaos depicted around him. Usually this cloud has faces of demons, puffs of dust, dangerous animals, fire, skulls, images of destruction. In yoga class the other day, as I lay in Savasana, I understood: This is the ultimate peace. To be able to sit stable in our sense of self as the world swirls and whirls around us. Without having to constantly please. Without having to constantly prove. Without having to follow all the trends. Without believing all the messaging bombarding us: *you are not okay, you are not okay, you are not okay.*

Everything changes. Nothing stays the same. This is what makes each wonderful thing so delicious and each terrible thing bearable. Nothing lasts. And yet . . .

We are taught from a young age that we have to change to be liked. We have to alter who we are to blend in and be accepted. So we learn to be chameleons. And we change color and shape to fit the needs and desires of those around us. Constantly. Until we no longer know who we are. What if we stayed true to who and what we are? Steady in it. What if we cultivated the best version of ourselves that we could and then trusted it? And owned it? What if we trusted that in our staying steady as self, those who dislike us would leave? What if we were okay with that? Knowing that those who love us would come? What if, in a world full of change and mystery, we knew we had our own back? That no matter what, we could trust ourselves to make the right decisions? That we would not abandon ourselves the way we did when we were children, when we were teenagers, when we were young adults in order to be loved. What if we gave *ourselves* everything we were yearning to have come from another? The acceptance. The love. The approval. The kind words. The presents. The gentleness and kindness. What if, like the Buddha in the thangkas, we could sit still and be at peace in the midst of the swirling chaos of the world? Wouldn't life be so much less scary? Wouldn't it be so much less disappointing? Wouldn't it be so much more fun?

Mahatma Gandhi once said, "It is better to be violent, if there is violence in our hearts, than to put on the cloak of nonviolence to cover impotence." This is how much *he* advocated being true to our real nature, even if our real nature is a nature of violence (which, when righteously aligned, is the nature of our warriors. Men and women who use the violence in their hearts to protect the weak and to stand up against those who would misuse their power in order to do others harm).

The process of publishing my book taught me to trust my voice. It taught me to own my story. It taught me if I was going to do it, I had to do it *my way*. Even if it "failed." No matter how many "experts" told me I was doing it "wrong."

The lifetime of betraying myself made me unable to betray myself a moment longer. The feedback became instant. I would spiral into depression the moment I tried. And as I stretch my wings and play with "how many yeses can I say before I have to say a no?" I continue to learn. I continue to discover what works for me and what does not. And as I honor, truly honor, what does work for me, I'm happier. I feel less of a need to impress my way, my views, onto others. I feel less of a need to condemn them for being different. And I am *so much* nicer to be around.

CHAPTER 34

Dichotomy

So many of us think we have to be one way all the time, have one consistent personality. More often than not it is a personality we created to please the world. As we got more and more positive feedback, we added more and more "approved behavior" to this personality. Which is exhausting and unsustainable. And yet the stripping of it, the dismantling of it, can, and often does, take us to the edge.

I have learned the hard way how important it is that we hold on to all sides of our personality.

When I was desperate to find God, to find my purpose, I struggled with the dichotomy within me. I yearned for God and was willing to do anything for freedom. In my journey toward enlightenment, I was willing to abnegate my own core essence when told to do so by my spiritual teachers. I was willing to shut down everything within me that I thought was "unspiritual." This was incredibly damaging.

I believe the dichotomy within us holds the answer. Is the answer. As Elizabeth Gilbert said so eloquently in *Eat, Pray,*

211

Love, "God dwells within you . . . as you. God's not interested in watching a performance of how a spiritual person looks and behaves. The quiet girl who glides silently through the place with a gentle, ethereal smile . . . who is that person? It's Ingrid Bergman in *The Bells of St. Mary's*—not me. God dwells within me . . . as me."

The enlightened version of each one of us is not some stripped down, boring, chaste dried-up sterile totally-not-fun monk woman/man wearing all white and a daisy behind our ear. The enlightened version is the loudest, brightest, most obnoxious version of us that we can come up with. Me, with all the skeletons in my closet dancing alongside me. You, with all the skeletons in your closet dancing alongside you. If we ever want true joy in our lives and on our planet, we must unleash the force within us. And . . . drumroll, please . . . it starts by owning our stories. Owning all of them. Not just the pretty pieces. The ugly pieces are undoubtedly as powerful as the glowing pieces. In fact, I would argue that they are more powerful. So let's excavate them. Let's drag them to the surface. Let's wash off the black sludge with a power hose, and let's hold those puppies up in the light. Let's look at them. Let's dissect them. Let's get the juice out of them, and then let's place them on the floor in front of us and bow low to them in gratitude. Yes, gratitude. Because they were our training. They were the backpack weighing fifty pounds that we strapped to our back as we ran up this mountain called life. The GREAT news is: we have done the training. Now it's time to reap the results and go out into the world and shine.

CHAPTER 35

FULL-BLOWN ALIEN

A friend of mine had suggested I watch the movie *Lucy* with Scarlett Johansson. He said it was about enlightenment. It was violent, and gory, and action-packed. But it was, in truth, about enlightenment. And it was also about being true to yourself.

Halfway through the movie I began crying. I hit pause and said to my friend, "This is the main question in life for beings like me . . . Do we keep trying to fit in? Or do we just eventually give up and go full-blown alien?" He looked at me and said, "You go full-blown alien." And we both laughed.

But I decided right then and there it was time to stop trying to blend in with other humans; it was time to *fully* be myself. So every moment of every day, I asked myself, "What would full-blown-alien Renee do right now?" Full-blown-alien Renee would not people-please. She would not alter her behavior in order to not offend. She was finally willing to be an outcast. Full-blown-alien Renee started writing what she wanted to write. She started saying what she wanted to say. She started dressing how she wanted to dress. She stopped being "nice" to people who were jealous of her or using her. And she completely gave up on dating humans. Because, of course, only another full-blown alien would suffice as a partner.

Full-blown-alien Renee came home one night from dinner with friends and wrote this: "Wanting/needing a man in my life severely disempowers me and makes me miserable. And it makes me a lost soul obsessing about something so much that I am cut off from life. This idea that I will only feel understood by this one man is a negative/false program that is putting my mind into hell. God/Goddess knows who I am and knows who will fit and is on it. I do not need to do anything. The only solution I can come up with is to completely drop the idea of a guy in my life. I do not need one. And instead allow in all the love and understanding from friends."

I decided to "date" my friends. I decided to get dressed up for them and to truly be present in every moment I spent with them (not scanning the room for my "partner"). I decided to finally *realize* that I had *so much love* and touch and divine companionship all around me all the time. I decided to luxuriate in all the partnership I *did* have. Without even realizing what I was doing, I radically shifted my vibration from "lack" to "abundance" when it came to the subject of partnership. I shifted from "don't have" to "do have." My heart went from empty and yearning to so completely full.

Holden appeared the next day.

CHAPTER 36

ROOM 444

Four has always been my lucky number. My favorite number. It was my father's and so it was mine. My father always saw the number four as a good omen. Every house we lived in had a four in the address.

After he died, I found out that four was his lucky number because in World War II, in the Battle of Elba, his was the fourth ship in line. The Germans had already arrived, catching the American ships by surprise and annihilating the first three. My father was able to turn his ship around and save everyone on board.

The first time I really used the money he left me was to buy a new car. A Volkswagen Jetta. I had a lot of guilt about buying myself a new car. I had always bought used junkers. (Which had broken down and left me stranded on the side of the road more than once.) When the license plate arrived, the first three numbers were 444. I cried. I knew my father was with me, and proud of me, and supportive of my choice to buy myself a safe vehicle.

When I was unsure about business schools and trying so hard to get into the right one, I noticed, after my interview with NYU, that the day was April 4 (4/4), the time of the interview was 4:00 p.m., on West Fourth Street, on the fourth floor, and my interview ended at 4:44 p.m. I ended up going to NYU.

And now, Holden. On the phone. Telling me to meet him in his hotel room because he had just gotten back from snowboarding and wanted to take a shower. His room number, he told me, was 444.

Of course it was. I mean, why would God/Goddess/Source send him from Japan to Glenwood Springs and *not* put him in room 444? I could feel all my nonphysical guides cheering.

And yet, meet him in his hotel room? *While* he's in the shower? Seriously? That did not seem like a good idea for multiple reasons. But I didn't worry about it. I knew I would get there after he was out.

When I was five minutes away, he called me. "Where are you?" he asked. I resisted the urge to mess with him. To say, "I'm sitting in room 444. Where are you?" just to see what his reaction would be. I decided not to. "Close," I said.

"Oh, okay. I left my jacket in my car, so I'm going to run down to the parking garage and get it. The door to my room is unlocked."

Here we go again. This guy really wanted me to already be in his room when he arrived to greet me. I told him I'd meet him in room 444.

So, I parked. And walked to the front of the hotel. And went in the lobby. But I didn't want to deal with reception calling him, so I immediately went up the lobby steps, to the top of the landing, which happened to be the third floor. I began to look for the elevator or more stairs. I walked past a set of double doors that went out to where my car was parked and took a few more steps down the hall, but felt it was a dead end and decided to turn around. When I did, a young man was walking toward me. He had on a tan/camo baseball hat, a brown jacket, and tan cargo pants. He was wearing a face mask, and I could only see his beautiful, brown, soft, kind, soulful eyes. He looked very young. Very handsome. Very strong. And very kind.

"Hi," I said. "Hi," he said back. We were the only two people around. It felt so quiet, as if time were standing still. And then he reached for the door handle. I saw the tattoos on his hands. Just as his face morphed into the Japanese partner I remembered from a past life. "Wait," I said. "Are you . . . you?" I asked him. The word *Holden* would not come. Because at that moment he was not just Holden. He was all the versions I had known him as in previous lives. "Yes," he responded. And his eyes smiled. What a weird question to ask someone: "Are you you?"

"I'm me . . ." he finished. He laughed as he said it.

I pulled down my face mask. "Holden, I'm Renee," I said. And then I hugged him. I couldn't help myself. I had to wrap my arms around him. I *remembered* him. Immediately. And he hugged me back. He held me. And we just stood there, wrapped in each other's arms. On the wrong floor. In the random spot that Source had decided would be our rendezvous point. Our reunion in the life.

I felt comfortable with him immediately. We walked to my car and began talking on the way to get something to eat. He began to tell me his story. And when we sat across from each other on the vinyl bench seats of a sticky booth in the Glenwood Springs Chili's, he began to tell me about his time in the military. He told me about how much he had loved his career. How hard it had been for him to be medically discharged. When I asked what he did in the military, he paused and then answered, "Military police."

I had found my Jack Reacher.

EPILOGUE

How cool is it that the same God that created
mountains and oceans and galaxies looked at you
and thought the world needed one of you too.

—ANONYMOUS

We are here by choice. On this planet by choice. In these bodies by choice. And we can leave anytime we want to. Seriously. Each day, each moment, each breath is a choice. Doesn't that truth change your perspective just a bit? We can leave whenever we want. But we took the time and made the effort to incarnate in a body and live all of this life so far, so why leave now? Why not stay and create a life we love? Have adventures? Do things that scare us? Go after what we want?

I think the greatest misunderstanding among humans is that once we die, life is over. This one belief system creates so much fear. And in our fear of dying, so many of us never truly live. I think quantity of life has become more important than quality. Our bodies are not meant to last forever. We are meant to transition out of them.

Albert Einstein once said the most important question we can ask ourselves is, "Do we live in a friendly or a hostile universe?" Why? Because our answer to this determines our life.

Too many of us have chosen "hostile." Have you noticed how we use martial language for everything? *The war on terror, the war on drugs, the war on cancer, the war on teenage pregnancy, the war on racism.* We even wage war against our own bodies with the "war on cellulite" or the "no pain, no gain" slogans we hear around exercise. Why are we always fighting? Why can't we trust that the Creator who made us knows what she is doing? What if we choose "friendly" instead?

We are here, on Earth, in these bodies, for such a short time. We are supposed to live in joy. We are supposed to discover and nurture and develop our divine gifts and share them with the world. We are not supposed to live in fear and lack and hatred and scarcity. These are all faulty belief systems that have been handed down to us and ingrained in us so deeply that too many of us created lives based on them. Our thoughts create our reality. If we believe life is hard and we live in a hostile universe, we create lives that reflect this.

We do not have to get married. We do not have to have kids. We do not have to buy huge houses with mortgages we cannot afford. We do not have to slave away at jobs we hate in order to pay for all these things. These are all *choices.* We owe it to ourselves to truly examine all the paradigms we have been handed by the collective and ask ourselves, "Does this make sense for *me*?" And if the answer is no, then it is time to disrupt these paradigms.

We are all unique. We are all here to express ourselves uniquely on our Earth Walk. Why do we keep choosing to build the same lives everyone else builds? We get married and wear the same color dress and buy the same type of ring and wear it on the same finger. Why? Because everyone else does. On Thanksgiving we buy the same foods and cook the same meals and eat them at the same time as everyone else. On a day that actually commemorates the slaughter of indigenous peoples. Why do we do this? Oh, because everyone else does. At Christmas we run around like crazy buying presents, too many of us hating this holiday. We do not have to do this. We have a *choice*. We do not have to participate in the consensus of mass consciousness.

When we are handed this one life to live (this time around), why are we holding back? Why are we not creating something magnificent and truly unique to us? Why are we coloring inside the lines? Why are we looking at what everyone else is painting and insisting on painting the exact same thing? When we have been handed a *totally blank* canvas!

The people we truly admire are the disruptors. The people who have truly "made it" are the disruptors. The ones who were willing to be outcast and ostracized in order to not follow the herd but to instead follow their own inner calling. These are the edge walkers. The leaders. They are willing to face ridicule and abandonment in order to truly shine in their authenticity. And always, once they have made their way, the people who ostracized and humiliated them suddenly want to worship at their feet. Always.

We have to be willing to follow the guidance of our heart. We have to be willing to wake up and walk our own authentic path. We have to trust in the Creator who made us, trust that we are never alone, and trust that we will always be guided when we learn how to slow down, get quiet, and listen within. True guidance sounds like love. It sounds like faith. It sounds like trust. It sounds like "everything will be okay, always has been, always will be." True guidance thrills our heart. It feels like inspiration. Anything else is fear-based confusion.

In a world this kind, if we get a disease, we stop and immediately ask ourselves, "Where am I stuck? Where am I resisting the flow of life? Where am I making self-destructive choices? Where am I not being true to the deepest calling of my heart? Where am I living out of alignment in order to please others, or because I am afraid to make changes?" And then we get still enough to listen to the answer. We thank the illness for waking us up. And we make the changes, which allows the life force energy to flood through our system once again and return us to the well-being that is our birthright.

In a world this kind, when crisis appears, we trust it and we look for the openings. We make the changes. We allow it to bring us to our knees, to undo us completely, to empty from our lives all that is being emptied, and then we rebuild a more authentic version of ourselves from the rubble. Only after the shattering is a rebuild possible.

I was free when I was traveling the world. I knew who I was before I joined that cult. Yes, I was searching, but only now do I realize I was already free. I was an extremely raw and authentic version of Renee. It took losing her completely. Trying to kill her. Covering her in all kinds of facades. Trying to turn her "holy." Burning all her belongings and crushing her surfboards with my car. Making her so miserable that she wanted to end her life. It took all of that to finally see that Renee knew who she was all along. And Renee needs no one in her life who does not empower, love, appreciate, and uplift her. No one.

And neither, my love, do you.

You must learn one thing. The world was made to be free in. Give up all the other worlds except the one to which you belong. Sometimes it takes darkness and the sweet confinement of your aloneness to learn anything or anyone that does not bring you alive is too small for you.

—DAVID WHYTE, *SWEET DARKNESS*

ACKNOWLEDGMENTS

When we speak we are afraid our words
will not be heard or welcomed.
But when we are silent we are still afraid.
So it is better to speak.

—AUDRE LORDE

Oh my gosh I have so many people to thank for encouraging me to speak! Well, to "write." Without them getting this book out into the world would not have been possible.

In no particular order—because each one was an integral part of creating this book—I have to thank Carrie W, who tirelessly read my manuscripts, offered comments and edits, and kept cheering me on. Sharon Goldinger of People Speak, my book shepherd and taskmaster who kept me on track and made sure I didn't birth into the world anything less than my best possible product. Mimi Bark for the beautiful cover and interior design; Penina Lopez for the wonderful editing; and James Gallagher for proofreading. Javier Perez of Page-Turner Publicity and Fauzia Burke of FSB Associates (and her amazing team Michelle and Anna) for helping me be seen and heard. John Burke for PubSite and for always being there to answer my questions. And thank you to Luann, Marla, and Carrie for reading my manuscript ahead of time and writing great blurbs.

I have to thank all the *amazing* men in these pages; without you I never would have learned to love. You truly were such magical, sparkly, handsome, sexy gifts in my life and I appreciate *each one of you* more than words can say. And last but most certainly not least I have to thank all of my friends. Without you life on Earth would not be worth living. You have been my tireless cheerleaders, always encouraging me, always understanding when I cancel plans because I'm in "Hermit Mode," never judging me, always helping me laugh at my mistakes. You make me smile and you fill my heart with so much *joy.* I love each and every one of you and feel so honored to call you "friend." Thank you for fanning my flames.

Set your life on fire,
seek those who fan your flames.

—RUMi

About the Author

© In Her Image Photography

Renee Linnell is a serial entrepreneur who has founded or cofounded five companies and has an MBA from New York University; before that she was a model and professional dancer. Her mission is to remind people Who They Truly Are and to reignite their passion for being alive. What began as writing for catharsis in 2013—as she struggled to regain her sanity after being brainwashed in a Buddhist cult—turned into her first memoir, *The Burn Zone: A Memoir* (She Writes Press, 2018). *Still on Fire* is the sequel. For more information, to read an excerpt of *The Burn Zone*, and to join her mailing list, please visit www.ReneeLinnell.com.